HAR DAYAL

Indian Freedom Fighters Series-52

Har Dayal

Role in Freedom Struggle

S.R. BAKSHI

Anmol Publications Pvt. Ltd.

New Delhi-110 002

ANMOL PUBLICATIONS PVT. LTD.
4374/4B, Ansari Road
Daryaganj, New Delhi-110 002

Har Dayal
First Edition 1994

ISBN 81-7041-706-6

PRINTED IN INDIA

Published by J.L. Kumar for Anmol Publications, Pvt. Ltd., New Delhi.
Printed at Renu Printers, Delhi.

Preface

Har Dayal, was a brilliant student who played a significant role in the freedom movement of India. He supported the revolutionary cult and functioned from Europe and U.S.A. for the cause of independence. His anti-Raj stance landed him into trouble at several occasions but his patriotic senti-ments never diminished rather his participation against the colonical rule became more magnified with the passage of time. He was a very fine speaker and could impress his audience with nice arguments. He always supported the socio-economic and educational standards of the people. He wrote several works and articles. Indeed he lived and died for independence for India.

I have collected the material from Nehru Memorial Museum and Library, Sapru House Library and Indian Council of Historical Research Library. I am grateful to the authorities of these institutions for helping me during my researches.

S. R. Bakshi

Contents

1

Early Career

Har Dayal played a most significant role in our freedom movement. He was born on 14 October 1884 in Delhi in a middle class family. His father, Gauri Dayal was a scholar of Persian and Urdu. Har Dayal received his education in Delhi, Lahore and Oxford. Indeed he was a brilliant student and received several awards during his student days. His memory was superb and could impress his audience with very nice performance. While he was in England, he was in touch with Dadabhai Nauroji, Savarkar and several other young patriots who were struggling hard for the independence of India. He had much respect for Tilak, Lajpatrai and Khaparde.

Har Dayal was a fine writer and through his writings he greatly influenced various sections of our society. Indeed his social and political ideas are clearly reflected in his writings. His correspondence with several patriots clearly show his working of mind. In fact throughout his career he had the anti—Raj stance. In U. S. A. and elsewhere he gave went to his feelings to larger audience about Indian nationalism.

32 Marina,
St. Leonards-on-Sea.
Aug. 28, '07.

Dear Sir,

I am sorry I have not received your letter of the 8th August which was sent to my college address. I have now received all letters that were detained during the last fortnight at Oxford, but your letter has not arrived among them. Kindly inquire what has become of it. I shall also make inquiries.

Kindly enroll the following among the subscribers to The Sociologist :

1. A. Sen, Esq., 41 Leamington Road, Villas, Bayswater, London W.
2. R. M. Khan, Esq., C/o Thomas Cook & Son, Ludgate Circus E. C.
3. B. L. Pasricha, Esq., C/o Thomas Cook & Son, Ludgate Circus, E. C.

I wish very much to see you in order to discuss with you the best way in which I can spend the next year. Two gentlemen have abandoned the professional studies they had come here for and are now staying with me for exclusively political study. They will study with me for a year for this purpose and intend to join the band of bhaktas. They have informed their parents of their patriotic resolve. I am considering if I should devote the next year to the study of the histor y of revolutionary movements. Indian economic and political problems and other subjects required for our movement and to the observation of the working of movements for freedom in Europe or to the preparation for Oxford B. A. degree. The latter seems to be a mere academic decoration for I must work for one year at the above-mentioned subjects before I can undertake active prachar among college students in India or be of some substantial use to the magazine. I cannot be a well-equipped Bhakta unless I study these subjects for one year. Now if I spend the next year in working for the Oxford degree, it might prove to be so much time wasted, for I have not got to take service anywhere or to parade my academic diplomas. An Oxford degree is no guarantee of such political knowledge as a bhakta of our movement should possess. Further I shall have to spend 3 or 4 months after my B. A. examination in travelling before I set to work studying the subjects connected with our movement. The political training of these two young gentlemen requires that I should attend to them and should form excellent epitomes out of the various books that I have read or shall read. One year is so much precious time in a revolutionary's life which is necessarily short and precarious.

I shall send you a complete Report on the question in a few days. I shall also ask you to enlighten me on the following points :

1. Do you approve of my giving up the University course and devoting myself to the work I have described ?

2. Could you still give me the Rs. 1000 which you have set apart for me now that I have resigned the Government Scholarship ? Of course, when you offered me that gift, the understanding was that I should work for B. A. degree. Now if I change my plan, could you continue the gift for the year under the altered circumstances ? If I come to the conclusion that I shall serve the Cause best by ceasing to cram for the University examination and devoting myself to real political study and observation, your gift will be returned to you unless you sanction its application for this new purpose. So please inform me if I may count upon your support to that extent in case I decide to give up the University course in favour of the other line of study. I have not arrived at a final decision yet, for I shall not decide till I have received your opinion as well as the opinions of other friends.

My idea is that I should return to India fully equipped for my work. If I take the Oxford B. A. degree, I shall have to study another year before I become a duly qualified bhakta. The two young men have abandoned all their studies and are reading Digby etc., and laboriously preparing themselves for the work of the propaganda.

The donor of the gold chain is Mr. Ram Lal, Hydro, Boars' Hill, (near Oxford). We are thinking of applying it for the purpose of the Prize for a Hindi poem on the Mahrattas. I hope you like this idea of us youngsters.

I have sent in my resignation of the Scholarship.

I hope the work is going on successfully at Paris.

S. Haidar Riza has also written to me about his idea. He wishes to join the Bar here. I have nothing to say in that matter as I do not know what correspondence has passed between you and him since I last met you.

Kindly inform me of your opinion as regard the course to be pursued by me during the next year. You can judge of the comparative utility of the two lines of study from the new considerations I have given above. And further, if you finally disapprove of the idea of giving up the University for the other work, could you continue your grant of 16 s. a week for the year in a case I come to the conclusion that I should give up the B. A. studies? I am pondering on this matter and pray that I may see my duty. I am afraid lest I may have my judgment warped by egoism or conventional modes of thought or vanity. I pray that I may see my duty and will act after due deliberation and consultation.

Mr. Jayaswal has sent you some sentences for The Indian Sociologist. Can I write something for The Indian Sociologist? Did you get my extracts from Thoreau's Civil Disobedience? I am glad they are holding regular weekly meetings at the India House. Could we make the institution more flourishing? Now that it is an eyesore for the Anglo-Indians, we should carry it to the highest pitch of success of which it is capable.

If you could give me the support to which I have referred above, I could spend a year in doing the following things :

1. Study of History of India, of Revolutionary Movements, of our own Problems etc.
2. Helping and guiding the two gentlemen in their studies and confirming them in their patriotic resolve by discourses. Already I talk to them an hour daily and they are encouraged by the practice. I want to make them pukka before they return at the year, lest they

should yield to the persuasions of their relatives. They have promised to spend a year in my company.

3. Travelling in England, Switzerland, Ireland and the U. S. America, observing the working of institutions and meeting representative workers in various movements.

4. Compiling the Text Books and Manuals of Indian Politics for our propaganda.

5. Helping Mrs. Chandu Lal in her political studies. (Mr. Chandu Lal is thinking of bringing his wife here to train her for the propaganda).

6. Writing for the Indian Sociologist.

7. Propaganda among such important young men as are in England.

Please give the matter your best consideration.

Yours very sincerely,
Har Dayal.

Oxford.
4. 11. '08.

Dear sir,

I am so pleased to read the suggestion you have made in your letter to Mr. Jayaswal. At present I am staying here with the help of Mr. Chandu Lal and Mr. Kashi Prasad Jayaswal. I have rented a bedroom. I get my meals at the house of friends. Some of the food I cook myself. Thus time passes in a very pleasant manner. Your good will has given me a great pleasure. Kindly don't worry about me.

The proclamation by the King has been published today.

A counterblast should be there in the Press. Now our party should send a manifesto by cable to India. It should consist of about two hundred words : a comprehensive answer to the proclamation besides suggestions.

If a cable is sent tomorrow or the day after it would be all right.

I have written to (B. C.) Pal that he should do his duty and have suggested a line of action. Still you should also send him a letter. You are already staying out. Why, therefore, should you not send a proclamation ?

If you think it advisable I can help you in drafting it. If you like you can let me have your opinion telegraphically.

Yours sincerely,
Har Dayal.

December 22, 1908.

The Editor,
The Indian Sociologist,
London.

Sir,

May I request the favour of your publishing the following ?

I owe it to my friends and acquaintances to explain my conduct in refusing to speak on any resolution at the Nationalist Conference held at Caxton Hall on December 20, and in leaving the meeting held on December 21 when Dr. Coomarswami was proposed to the chair. As regards the Conference I may inform your readers that I was asked by the organisers to speak on the resolution of Boycott. I accepted the duty with pleasure. But when I learned that Mr. Parkeh was also to be invited to take an active part at the meeting, I at once refused to appear on the same platform with a person who was a Hindu but who has been converted to Christianity since his arrival in England under certain circumstances which are known to all.

I am very happy that I decided to hold aloof from the work of the Conference for I was surprised in the evening to find that the resolution on swaraj was entrusted to a certain Dr. Coomarswami (of whom more anon) and that the list of speakers included men who have married English women and Mohammedans who are so patriotic as to eat beef. I am glad that I was spared the pain of supporting such a programme.

I was told that the organisers of the meetings for Mr. (Bepin Chandra) Pal's lectures intended to ask Dr. Coomarswami to preside on the evening of December 21. Now this gentleman is a Eurasian and has married an English-woman although he possesses an Indian name and wears a turban. As soon as I realised that it would injure our movement if we elected such a man to preside at a nationalists, meeting I held back.

In order to avert the impending calamity I informed the organising secretaries that I intended to propose some other lady or gentleman when Dr. Coomarswami's name should be put forward by those who desired that he should preside. But I was informed by one of the secretaries that the meeting had been convened by certain persons, and that the proceedings would be conducted according to a programme that had been laid down by them. I was also given to understand that these meetings were not "public" meetings in the sense that everything was to be submitted to the meeting for approval and that I would not be justified, as a mere member of the audience, in making a counter-proposal on the question of the election of president. I suggested that if the meeting approved of Dr. Coomarswami's election, the organisers would lose nothing but that if the majority disliked the idea after listening to my arguments, it was unfair to take advantage of their ignorance of Dr. Coomarswami's antecedents and force a Eurasian on them for president. I thought that I should be allowed to propose some other lady or gentleman and to explain my reasons for doing so. The meeting could decide. But as this alternative was rejected by the organising secretary, I realised the force of the saying that those who paid the piper had the right to call the tune. I then considered it dishonourable to make any counter-proposal; I had, therefore, no choice but to enter a silent but eloquent protest against the whole affair by leaving the Hall, where great discourses on Nationalism are delivered under the presidency of Eurasians who marry English-women.

I am all the more happy that I did so, as I learned afterwards. I was also much pained to learn that Mr. Ratcliffe was requested to address the meeting. Is he an Indian or does he support the ideal of the absolute independence of India?

I shall be glad if nationalists would express their views on these questions, so that there may be no mis-understanding in the future.

Yours sincerely,
Har Dayal.

29, Poplar Grove,
Shepherd's Bush, W.
December 22, '08.

10 Avenue Ingris,
Passy,
Paris.
February 2, 1909.

Dear brother Har Dayal,

Bande Mataram,

I received your postcard. Your letter, however, reached me last evening. You have stated about your health. It is clear that the climate of a cold country does not suit you. In my opinion it is not proper for you to stay on in Europe. Your trouble will aggravate in cold clime; it might assume the form of consumption. This is what the doctor says. A friend of mine was in a similar condition. He began to spit out blood. His doctor pressed upon him to leave England and go back to his native land. I would advise you to take care of your body first. Only through body can one realise dharma (duties), artha (wealth,) kama (desires) and moksha (emancipation). You can regain health by going back to India and living among your relatives and friends there. You know that in this country one has to spend much on board, lodging and other things whereas in our country one can manage these things in a smaller amount.

When you were in the Punjab, I had written to you that you should come to London and manage the India House. But you did not agree to this, even after you had reached London. If you had managed the India House and given moral instructions to the inmates off and on you would not have undergone expenditure on food and clothing and I too would have been spared the botheration. Now you want £ 80 every year. I am sorry I cannot give this amount. This year I have spent about one hundred on the repairs of the India House. Again, you know I have given away rupees five thousand to the Indian Martyrs' Memorial. At the present moment, therefore, I cannot undertake to give away any more money as charity. In connexion with The Indian Sociologist I have to spend £ 125 on printing, salary of a clerk and the like. For the sake of country too, I have to set apart an amount every year. You have suggested that donations should be invited. I don't like to ask anybody for a donation. I donate whatever I can myself. You write to your friends whatever you think proper. I set apart the amount of 500 for you. Out of it about £ 18 are there with me. When you go back to India you can take this from me. This will help you for your passage. Mr. Kashi Prasad Jayaswal passed on a certain amount to be spent through you. Out of it £ 10 are there. I hope Mr. Jayaswal would give this sum to you.

In going back to India there is the fear of tortures at the hands of the English. But in living here there is the fear of death itself. You do that which is less harmful. Now the time of violent speeches or writings in India is gone. If, therefore, you shun agitating violently, I am sure, you will have no danger from the English.

Kindly ponder over these things. If, however, you want to stay in this cold country you write to me and I send you the allotted sum. You have asked for £ 10. If you like I can send this sum.

Kindly write to me about your health. Bande Mataram to all friends.

Yours sincerely,
Shyamaji Krishnavarma.

Albergo Isola Bella,
Salsomaggiore.
August 9, 1909.

Dear Mr. Rana,

Your letter to hand. I am sick of Shyamaji's egoism. The question raised by Das did not seem to arise out of what we had written. There was no discussion of the claims of leaders etc. We said that the name was borrowed because the work of Calcutta Bande Mataram was carried on advanced lines. We do not want to be involved in personal quarrels. The paper (Bande Mataram) is for discussion of principles and not for praising or dispraising individuals in an invidious fashion. Those who do not want to work but always regard their selves had better betake themselves elsewhere. Even if anybody attacks us personally I am not going to reply. For our space is valuable and we shall only disgust our youths if we even reply to attacks on us. What they want is food—mental and moral, and ideas and instruction. They don't want either eulogy or condemnation of Shyamaji or yourself or myself apart from political views etc.

What hurts Shyamaji is not this, but the very fact of our paper being started. He is, as I have told you, not patriotic but at bottom egoistic or cowardly too. Now people will see the difference between our paper, full of sound articles and notes and free from personal self-advertisement, and his Indian Sociologist which was not a nationalistic organ so much as a medium of gaining notoriety for Shyamaji. That was its main function. You see his idea is that he should be the only "boss" He is not patriotic but selfish under the mask of patriotism. I have put him beyond the pale of co-operation in my estimation as he is incurably vain, greedy, tortuous and selfish.

He typifies the vices which have brought us down. And someday he could inaugurate the movement !

At any rate, our paper is not for individual quarrels. We have not said if Tilak or Aurobindo or Dayanand or who began the movement. That does not concern us. I again repeat my idea that we should have nothing to do with him but let him work as he likes, for I cannot know how you can work with an entirely egoistic man, whose word you can't trust.

I shall send The Bande Mataram to Cambridge in another way. I had sent another parcel to another student which has reached him. This one was returned by the college as they saw its contents. Perhaps the addressee was away for vacation and the college examined the contents.

Yes, we shall post from England to India. The best plan is to give our supporters in England several copies each and ask them to send to their friends. Thus they will each spend something on postage out of their pockets. We always sent The Indian Sociologist this way. I have sent parcels to many students in London, with the request that they should send copies in letters to their friends and return all undistributed copies to me.

Have you been corresponding with Savarkar ? We should now know about his plans.

Thanks for regular supply of newspapers. I am coming in December as soon as Mr. (Chandu) Lal leaves for India, as in the absence of company and the amusement of Paris streets, my nerves are getting strained. Besides, the work of editing can be more easily done from there. I don't believe it is absolutely necessary for me to pass winter in South. It is good from the point of view of health but then there is the question of loneliness. So I have decided to come in December.

Mrs. (Chandu Lal is better but really she can't recover here. She has to pass the next two months somehow. India will do her good. She can't get proper food and company and climate here. Mr. Lal will return to Oxford for his examination and I shall take her to Beaulieu near Nice. More again. Is le plus grand homme come back ? My Bande Mataram to Mrs. Rana.

Yours affectionately,
Har Dayal.

I enclose a letter to Mrs. Cama. You can also read parts of this letter to her.

As to subscription, I expect every Indian in Paris will give 5 francs a year at least and more ardent men like Godrej etc. will give at least 5 francs a month. Have a small box made for collecting subscriptions and let them put the money in. I shall go round collecting from time to time. You'll see we shall get much in this way.

I send you the Postal Order. Tell me what you think of (Kashi Prasad) Jayaswal's affair.

C/o Thomas Cook & Sons,
Bon Port,
Montreux (Switzerland).

My dear Bhaiji, (Parmanand)

Gobind Chand and others at Oxford do lots of debating but say one thing and influenced by their old customs, do something else. The time is passed for comfortable politics.

Yours affectionately,
Har Dayal."

Pension Du Midi,
San Remo (Italy).
October 18, 1909.

Dear Mr. Rana,

I have heard from Shri Savarkar. I hope he is now in Paris. He likes The Bande Mataram. He suggests that

Deshbandhu should be used instead of Shriyut. It is a good suggestion and I accept it.

We have come here from Salsomaggiore. It is a warm place but there are many mosquitoes. We are lucky in getting a pension at 5 francs a day. It is a good maison and we are very comfortable. I had thought the Riviera would be very expensive. Mrs. Lal is improving. We had an examination a few days ago and her lungs are much better. The temperature is also lower, and she has gained in weight. I am glad this is so, as she is a valuable worker and has been trained for work among ladies in India, and her returning to India as a malade would have produced a bad impression on other youths who may be thinking of bringing their wives to Europe like Mr. (Chandu) Lal and myself. I believe she will continue to improve now, and there is no anxiety.

I am very happy that you settled the matter with Shyamaji in this way. I am glad he excused himself and denied any intention of injuring you. I hope his calumnies against you will cease new, though I rather doubt it. Anyhow you have done your duty as a gentlemen in telling him in a friendly way about it. I hope he will behave himself better in future. I should have been amused to see how he looked when you told him of the "psychological murder." That was a good idea.

By the by, you take too exaggerated a view of these things as regards me. What is the "storm" that may break out against me and the "clouds" etc. ? Shyamaji's slanders and womens' talk are of no importance. I don't know how his remarks about me can injure me, for I have no worldly interests that could be attacked (e. g. post, wealth, house etc.), and my studies and my moral ideas no one can deprive me of. As to other peoples' opinion about me, I don't care and besides I am above slander, as everyone who know's me loves me. So this ebullition of wounded vanity on Shyamaji's part need not trouble us. He doesn't like me because I did not think it proper to ask him for help after he had once shown himself mean and selfish. That I can't help. If he is mean, I cannot change my opinion of his character to please him and I cannot accept his money, be it however small a sum, when I know that he does not give it as a comrade a colleague contributing something to the work that I do but as a patron giving something to a man who begs a charity for himself as he is in difficult circumstances. That's his feeling, and therefore, I did not want his money. I have not rid myself of all worldly ties and obligations to be patronised by fellows like him. So you need not trouble yourself much about his fulminations, as I can't change my opinion about him and I cannot, therefore, act towards him as if I esteemed him. So his complaint will always go on. As to reforming him, I find it out of my power, unless indeed he falls very ill or find himself in some difficulty in which Money will not avail him but the help of human love. Then I can prove to him by my service that the Money which he values is nothing and that mutual love, which he knows nothing about, is everything. But that is going away too far from the present. Please find out in conversation why exactly he is angry with me. I don't know that I have injured him. I think it is only wounded egoism. What is your impression ?

If Savarkar is in Paris, please let me know his address. I shall write to him.

You may keep Shroff's postal order, as I can cash it in Paris in December when I come, as Shroff may find it troublesome to have it refunded to himself after having once sent it away to me. You can keep it, as it's available for one year.

The magazine has cost 60 francs (50 fr. for printing and 10 for Postage.) A little more postage may be spent afterwards.

please send me £ 20 as early as passible. Sorry to trouble you so often. Do you think I shall be able to find a pension for 4 or 4½ or 5 francs a day (inclusive) in some part of Paris in December ? I think one should not live in suburbs in winter. Please see if you come across any advertisement etc. From what I gathered about Mr. Nageeenawala's pension and Mrs. Cama's, I thought Paris was a dear place. Kindly be on the look-out for advertisements. I read the advertisements in The

Daily Mail only.

Tell me criticisms and suggestions of friends on the December number of The Bande Mataram.

My respectful Bande Mataram to Mrs. Rana and fondest love to Ranji.

Please don't fail to write to me of Savarkar's address in Paris if he has arrived.

Yours affectionately
Har Dayal.

Senor Ferrer's affair has rather upset my sleep this week. Otherwise I am all right. Why don't Indians assemble in London to condemn the Spanish Government like all advanced bodies? I doubt if anyone can convene a meeting in London. What do you think?

Poste Restante,
Alger,
7 May, 1910.

Dear Mr. Rana,

I arrived on Thursday late in the evening after a sail of 46 hours. The Boat was slow on account of a rough sea. I was ill all the way.

I like the town, as it reminds me of Bombay. One sees the oriental dress and barefoot people and veiled ladies and summer clothing. I am keeping good health. The clothes I am wearing are too warm. So I am going to get summer stuff such as the Arabs wear pretty much the same as we have in India but looser.

Please send me newspapers etc. to the above address. But kindly spell my name always as "Har Dayal".

What have you found in papers? I hope Jayaswal has returned from London.

The scenery over the gulf is magnificent.

Alger is a winter fashionable resort. Many English and American people come and live in the first class hotels in Mustapha quarter in winter. You and Mrs. Rana can come for a trip, if you find time. I shall have the pleasure of seeing you here : so the advice is not altogether disinterested. But it is good all the same.

I have met our Indian friends for whom Nageenawala gave me the letters. They seem to be good people. There are about ten Indians in the place all told, though I have so far been only four of them.

The town has all the characteristics of French life. There are too many cafes and bars, though.

I am beginning to learn Arabic. My stay in Algerie will give me a good opportunity of learning Arabic and Islamic history and religion. So I begin at once.

There is a sort of bibliotheque : so I can go on with my French. But there is not much on other subjects. The town is full of the riffraff of Italy and Spain and Greece, who come here to make money.

More again.

Yours affectionately,
Har Dayal.

Hotel de la Californie,
Rue Charlemagne,
Alger.
Friday (May 14, 1910).

Dear Mr. Rana,

Glad to here from you. I am staying here for a month. After that, I have already arranged in a village nearby. I am well now, though I was a little indisposed for several days. How did Mme Cama's soiree go off? Please tell Madame Rana that I am waiting for her letter.

I remember Ranji and Madame Rana very much. Do they also remember me or not ? Has Ranji got his book from Perrin ? And my big over-coat ?

Kindly send me Indian newspapers as soon as you can, as I have to get up the MSS. (for The Bande Mataram).

I am all right. I write a lot to little Perrin. Those who want all details should ask her.

Yours affectionately,
Har Dayal.

The place is good but very noisy and the hotel-proprietress is very dishonest. The other place in the village is better.

Hotel de la Californie,
Rue Charlemagne,
Alger.
May 19 (1910).

Dear Madame Rana,

I am waiting for your letter in reply to the one that I wrote to you. I hope you will write soon. Want of time is no excuse in this case.

I am getting on very well. You need not be anxious on my account. The town and its suburbs are very interesting. I made the acquaintance of two Arab students, but they seem to wish to thrust their services on me as teachers of Arabic. I shall not, therefore, cultivate their society much. I don't know their character. I am making progress with French and Arabic. There are two public libraries, where I go every day to study.

I have not mixed much with our Indian compatriots here as I wish to cultivate the habit of living alone and to suppress the hankering for social intercourse which is after all a weakness. I shall take care that my health does not suffer. With that reservation, I shall try to dispense with company as much as possible.

This town is almost European, as the Arabs are nearly one-fifth, as numerous as the Europeans. Later on I may go further South, where the Arab population predominates.

The weather is mild and pleasant. We keep the windows open at night. I have already enjoyed the luxury of going out without socks ! It reminds me so much of India.

I hope you remember me on Sunday morning at de jeuner time.

Ranji must have got his Gospel of Buddha from Perrin. Please read it with him often from beginning to end. Even if he doesn't understand many things now, that doesn't matter. It is my firm conviction that every young man be taught to have a serious view of life and firm religious principles which form the basis of his character. For religion alone teaches us to be good and honest and truthful and self-denying, and religion alone gives us strength in the hour of trial. So you should not neglect to give Ranji a thorough grounding in religious principles as illustrated in the lives of founders of religions. Later on I well send Ranji a copy of Thomas a Kempis's Imitation of Christ, a book of the highest value for the formation of character.

How is everybody doing ? I write very often to little Perrin about every detail that I find interesting. I am afraid there might be danger for her if she goes back to India. I miss your company and hers so much !

How is Jayaswal getting on ? You can write to me here to my hotel address up till the 4th June. After that I shall go to Et Biar, a village near Alger. Or you may find it convenient to retain the permanent address, Poste Restante, Alger.

I am eagerly waiting for your letter.

With best wishes,

Yours sincerely,
Har Dayal.

Hotel de la Californie,
Rue Charlemagne,
Alger.
May 19, 1910.

Dear Mr. Rana,

I am all right. If you can send some newspapers, please do so. I am getting on with my regular routine.

I find the town and its suburbs interesting. But it is all just like Europe. These peoples have colonised so quickly! For pure Arab towns, one must go south, where the number of Europeans is small.

I am making progress with Arabic.

How is everybody going on in Paris?

What about our friend the Tailleur?

Yours affectionately,
Har Dayal.

Letter No. 20 : In this letter to Mrs. Rana Har Dayal says he is "searching the Principle of Good. . . and Love. . . in this world of Evil and Grief and Suffering."

Poste Restante,
Alger.
Sunday.

My dear Madame Rana,

Pardon me that I do not come to see you all before going away. My heart really aches to see you all. I cry several times a day, especially when I am taking my meals all alone. But if I come I am afraid I shall cry and may wish to stay in Paris. On account of many trials and struggles, my heart has become weak and hungry. In February 1909, the doctor, after examining me, said : "This heart has suffered almost to breaking-point. It might have burst any time during the last six months, and you might have died of heart-failure." So if

I come now, my overburdened heart, which seeks repose and sympathy, may conquer my resolution, and I may fail to carry out my plan of going away. I cannot trust my will now. The pain will be greater than the pleasure, and the second separation will be too much for me. Therefore I wish to go away from here directly.

I have read several good French books here: Chateaubriand's Les Martyrs and Rene and Atala, Victor Hugo's L' Armee Terrible and others.

Kindly always write to me lovingly, for I am going into the "friendless waste", lonely, and letters from those who love us are a great boon.

I sail on Friday the 17th instant. I shall write to you again before departure.

Don't worry about me. I shall take care of myself, and hope to see you all in a better world.

Ever your own wandering boy,
Har Dayal.

Don't write to me till you hear from me from America.

P. S. I received your loving letter after I had written the above. You should not worry so much. If occasion offers, I may come to see you all some time. I am stopping till December in America, I think, to wait for some things and develop some plans. Then I shall decide if I should go on to Japan or not. I am not going straight to Japan. Now if I stop in America, that will not be very far. The mail comes in a week, and you can write often. And after some years, I can come on a holiday in France to see you all. It is probable that I shall not reach Japan. Everything depends on circumstances. I can say nothing for certain. Now if I do not go to Japan but remain in the United States, that will not be so bad after all. Don't you think so ?

I shall take care of health, especially cold and overwork.

And I shall try the mandoline, and find and or two friends where I go. Do not worry about me at all. I shall be quite all right, and shall work happily wherever I am. Pray do not worry. I search the Principle of Good and Comfort and Love and Peace in this world of Evil and Grief and Suffering. So sweeten my work by your letters and don't worry. Don't worry. Don't worry. That's all I can say.

Letter No. 21 : It appears that the Ranas press Har Dayal again and again to return to Paris. Har Dayal in reply says : "I cannot return. How I wept on leaving it. I leave half my heart behind me".

Post Restante,
Alger.

Dear Mrs. Rana,

Many thanks for your kind words. I do not know how to reply to you.

Paris was for me a place of rest and quiet and study and good society. But I assure you that I cannot return. How I wept on leaving it ! I leave half my heart behind me. I leave behind me the only friends I have at present.

If I could return, there would be no need of your asking me to do it. I should have come back myself. But as you do not know why I have left Paris, you cannot form an opinion in this matter. Leave it to me. Yes, I am mechant and ungrateful not to obey you. But I assure you that my destiny takes me away from you and all the friends in Paris and from my work there.

I shall write to you whenever I may be. I do not know what may happen to me in future. But I shall never forget your kindness to me. I owe you more than I can ever repay. And I shall ever think of you with reverence and gratitude.

Best love to Ranjit.

I leave on the 10th if my others arrive in time; otherwise on the 17th. If you write, please write C/o Poste Restante now.

Yours ever sincerely,
Har Dayal.

Hotel La Californie,
Alger.
Monday, 8 a.m.

Dear Mr. Rana,

I am much better now, though I often find relief in crying. It is good for me.

To the number of those to whom information is to be sent, if my work on this wretched earth is ended within the next five years, please add the following :

(1) Hamed el Alaily, Damietta, Egypt.

(2) Arnold Freeman, B.A., 6 Woodberry Down, London N.

(3) M.L. Gourmah, C/o Hamed el Alaily, Damietta.

I have strong presentiment that I shall drop and so end. Dr. Femet told me to be "habitually gay", but I think I shall find it very hard to be gay even at long intervals. If my important plan succeeds, I shall have a source of joy and consolation and comfort in that. But I am not hopeful about its success. I am afraid it will not take practical shape. I have tried my mandoline. But it brings no gaiety. I put it by. Perhaps after some time, I shall find it more serviceable.

I pray you not to speak or think unlovingly of me on account of my going away. I am myself quite unnerved and unmanned by the step. And dark fears hover over my soul. Like a shady tree to the weary traveller in the heat of the noon, like the chink of light in the wall of the dark cell to the prisoner, so was your home to me at this critical period of my life. I only say with Job, "The Lord gave and the Lord took away. Blessed be the name of the Lord." So I pray you not to speak or think harshly of me in your home. I would be heart-broken, if you did not bear this in mind. Give me your promise.

Fondest love to Ranji.

Yours ever affectionately,
Har Dayal.

P. S. I read in the paper that 33 confessions have been made in the Naski trial ! That is terrible.

I leave on the 17th. I shall send the MSS for the July number of The Bande Mataram before going. If you get The Punjabi please send it to me. Also the new Modern Review. I shall send it back.

Again, I assure you that it is not from anger or unworthy resentment or any feeling of that sort that I go. Believe me in this. I have not the habit of lying. I recognise that I should go, that the time has come for me to go. Everything has an end, and why not my stay in Paris ? I see that our views differ, that our ideas, differ, that our plans differ. I see this, and it is time for me to go. There is no other way out of the difficulty : there is no other solution of the question. Don't you see this too ? I am touched with your great love and your sweet good nature, your thorough disregard of self in this matter. I see that you are so good and noble in asking me to come back.

But I recognise that though our hearts are one, our ideas are different. Don't you feel this, Mr. Rana? So I do not think that I go out of a mere fancy or passing feeling. No. I recognise that we do not look at things in the same way, and my stay in Paris would create awkward situations and useless difficulties in future for the small group of Nationalists there. I do not wish to put you and others in those difficulties. I have my own whims and fancies, my own foolish dreams and ways of work. Why should I create needless entanglements for you in future by persisting in living in Europe or Paris ? I would be a constant source of difficulty, an ever present stumbling block for others. So I wish to eliminate myself, calmly, deliberately. I am touched deeply with your uniform good nature and patriotism, your humility and modesty. But why should I make my peculiar whims and ideas a cause of evil for the Paris group of Nationalists ? You are right and wise in asking me to stay. I am right and wise in going. Let both do their duty in this way. I hope you will perceive the truth of what I have said.

And if, in the moments of irritation in these last days, I may have uttered words which showed that I went away in anger, pray do not take those words as the expression of my true sentiments. My mind is a hell, and my heart has had to suffer great trials. Therefore I am entitled to indulgence. And so in moments of temporary irritation, I may have showed vexation. But that is not the feeling in my heart. I go because I realise that I should go for the benefit of the party and that my stay would injure it in future. That's all.

My spirit has not the constant gentleness of a perfect man. I am young and have not achieved complete self-conquest. Consider this, and do not take occassional words of vexation as the expression of my feelings.

Of course, the heart-pain remains. Love claims its due. But that is a different thing altogether.

To you I owe nothing but kindness ! Remember that my heart has undergone trials which would have made another man reel and stagger. Though I am only 26, my heart has experienced all the gamut of human feeling. The suppression of the natural filial, fraternal, conjugal and paternal feelings, the total estrangement from all early friends whom I loved as the light of eyes, the rupture with all the family, the incompletion of my academic studies at Oxford, and the waste of endeavour, the sudden interruption of my magnificent apostolic work in India on account of the bomb affair, and then the fruitlessness of all my labour in training my wife and the preachers and the disappearance of all that I had done, the constant contemplation of the misery of our country,—then illness and—that which cut me to the quick—begging from father-in-law, from brother, from Shyamaji ! And physical collapse and ruin of my splendid nervous system ! And—worst of all—the abandonment of my austere idealistic habits for the restoration of my over-wrought nervous system, the putting away of the yellow turban, the wandering of thoughts to amusement and frivolity, the loss of twenty per cent of my hard-earned moral strength. So there you see me—the body ruined by the hard work and thought, which resulted in nothing on account of the bomb affair : the Moral Gain, the result of hard religious training and struggle, lost to prop up this body,—what a complication of calamities ! And the body is still unrestored ! May life be cursed ! And the Result is Nothing ! And the heart is sick, empty, hungry !

And last of all, now the perception that the task is very great and I am as yet incompletely equipped for it ! When I arrived in Europe in September 1908 I was more inclined to teach : now I am more inclined to learn ! I now see how much I have to study and learn before I can set up as a teacher.

And then the humiliation of money-entanglements ! When I began my preaching in India, I bade goodbye to all money-complications. I thought I was happy. And now again those entanglements ! Alas ! the bomb has upset all my plans of work; it has thrown confusion into all my firmly-based life-structure. I don't know if I can balance the good and the evil of it. I say it was very premature.

And again now arise dark doubts about life and its meaning, about the possibility of the triumph of good. And over all looms the question of improving my Personality, without guide, without help, without sympathy, without love. A dreary struggle !

And now the anxiety about future work ! You solved the whole thing by saying that there was only literary work to do! Alas ! it is not so easy. Mere literary work is useless. Workers are not produced like that. Virtues are not implanted by economic histories of India. If I should content myself with that idea, all my past work would be wasted, all my struggle fruitless, and no permanent good can result in future. No, I will struggle on, though at present I am a prey to conflicting emotions. I will not rest on the lower steps of the temple, merely because I find myself in Europe. The body will be restored after some time. And if it is not, let it perish. I cannot yield up to its demands everything for which I have devoted my youth. It will die now near the ideal rather than live away from it !

I write all this to relieve my own heart, for feelings poured out before a loving friend, give relief. If any other man had passed through all this, he would have stumbled and fallen, never to rise again. But thanks to my Master, the ever gracious, the ever-conquering Lord Buddha, the Soul of all souls struggling with evil, the Prince of those who have loved mankind. Yes, thanks to my gentle, loving, all-wise Master, whose voice I hear across the centuries, I have not lost my hold on the great principles of the good life, of the Higher Life. Only twenty per cent loss has been sustained. And one item of loss is that my soul is not so gentle and sweet now as it was, as it should be.

You and Madame Rana have done me nothing but good. And I cherish the liveliest remembrance of your goodness and modesty. So I wish to part in perfect sweetness and peace.

So my dear Mr. Rana, my whole life is hanging in the balance. The dreams of my youth, the visions of my life, for which I have struggled and fought with myself during nights of weeping and prayer, are fleering before me. No—I will not lose all that which is the only reward that I have got for my almost super-human efforts of self-suppression. I have sold family and peace of mind and everything, and got something in return. That something is my yellow turban.

Alas! during the fifteen months (since February 1909, when I fell ill), I have made health my chief and primary consideration. I have subordinated every other thing to it. I have put the restoration of my nervous system as the great object of life. But now I am weary of this search for health and strength. It has made me upset all the pillars of my life. It has exposed me to humiliations, inconsistency, moral degradation. It has sullied the purity of mind with thoughts of frivolity. It has made me seek amusement and enjoyment. It has robbed me of my yellow turban. It has dragged me down. It has marred the perfect selflessness of my friendship for my wealthy comrades. It has introduced evil worldly elements into my relations with my dearest of friends. It has made me think of money, of my body, of the future.

It has degraded and debased and demoralised me. O my God! I cannot pay all this price for the nervous system. I will not pay it any longer. Let health and struggle come, or let them not come. Let sleep come or let it not come. Let headache remain or go away. Let the appetite be good or bad. I must cease to care for all this. One year of this left has been enough for me. For health, I have sacrificed too much. I cannot sacrifice it any longer. I don't care if a strong constitution comes or does not come. Now I am content. Now I have cut at the root of the cause of my misery during the past year. I am here giving you, Mr Rana, the innermost thoughts of my heart, the thoughts on which I have brooded and which have rent my heart during the past six months. I look back on my past life during five years and I weep, weep! The ruin of my glorious work in India, the ruin of several youthful lives, and the interruption of my carefully drawn-up propaganda for the Cause in Northern India gave me much pain. But what shall I say as to the consequences of my physical breakdown? They are source of pure agony. But now it is all right. I have sunk low, I have compromised the purity of my soul, I have thought of money and comfort. Oh, I have lost a part of the great reward of my struggles, in the search of health and strength. But now I will not pay all this price. I will not lose the result of days of toil and nights of waking for this object : I will not stoop to conquer health. I have lost enough of my moral gains in this attempt. Let health come or go.

I don't care for this blesssed nervous system any longer.

So, Mr. Rana, let me go. My heart is full. It is bruised. broken, hungry, aching. The fruit of all my gigantic efforts is escaping from my grasp. I am becoming mean, low, bitter, frivolous, worldly, demoralised. I am becoming entangled in the bog of money-matters and amusement, which means death to my dreams, death to my ideals, death to all which I have striven with heroism. Desire for health has caused all this. I now abandon that desire.

Like unto a vessel tossed by a storm in the dark night, so I am. Write to me lovingly, for my heart craves for love, for sympathy. It is wounded, wounded, wounded.

The whole of this has been written while weeping.

Show this last piece to Jayaswal too. It will convince him that I should go.

Hotel de la Californie,
Rue Charlemagne,
Alger.
Monday. 11 a.m.

Dear Mr. Rana,

I have already written to you a long letter today, pouring out my heart to you like a child. So never think that I am forgetful of all your kindness to me. You and Madame Rana have given me my life back again, by endangering your own and that fact alone will be your title to my gratitude for ever. I say all this to assure you of my sincere feelings. It will be a great blow to my heart if you think that I for whom you have done so much, have at the end gone away in anger or grief or disappointment. No. Grief there is, for my heart craves for the love and sympathy, which I could find in Paris. But that is a different thing.

You see, if I stay on, I shall be always entangled in the bog of money-matters in one way or the other. Either I shall make money—from which temptation Heaven save me. For

I have already come back a long distance on the path, on which I was so successfully advancing to moral glory when I fell ill. But there are two gates which mark the boundary line between the ordinary life that I have left and the higher life which I love. I will not re-enter these gates even for health. They are : (1) Money-making, (2) Sexual intercourse even with my wife. I have stooped to frivolity, sight-seeing, gossip, reading tales and novels and indolence in order to soothe my heart-pain and relieve my nerves and get good sleep and appetite. But how far shall I go on falling for health and strength? Fifteen months I have wandered in this wilderness. I have now determined to abandon the care for health and strength, that is, to cease making it the primary object of my endeavours. Let the thing go on as it can.

Or if I don't make money, I shall continue to introduce evil elements into my friendship with my comrades. Oh, how I hate all money-making! How my heart is upset by these entanglements. It is as if a man, who had run away from a lion, should see him again standing before him. And then I feel degraded and wretched. I care only for the welfare, moral and mental, of my friends and ask only for their love in return, but they may think that I cling to their money! How the idea haunts me, breaks my heart. No, this kind of thing will never do. If I stay on in Paris now, my whole life will be poisoned. The desire for strength as a means of working for others has caused me up till now to trouble my comrades and ask for their help. But now I abandon that desire. It is the source of moral evil than good, as I have shown you in my last letter. It makes my life very similar to that of a charlaton like Pal! Oh God! what a termination of my labours! No, Mr. Rana, you are my friend. My heart is already wounded, bleeding and pierced. If I live in Paris, I shall pine away and die, as I have already written to you. The burden on the heart will be too much. I shall go mad or pine away. It is not possible for me to come back. Write to me always, you and Madame Rana. I have asked Perrin also to write to me always. Tell me all about dear Ranji from time to time, how he is making progress and growing in grace and favour. Tell me everything in your letters. That will sweeten my life. That will at least give me some of that love and sympathy, for which my heart is hungry, oh so hungry, in its present bruised and bleeding condition.

I love you and Madame Rana and our dear Ranji the same as ever. But I cannot return to live there.

Ever yours affectionately,
Har Dayal.

Always write to me lovingly, very sweetly.

You can show this to Jayaswal too. It will convince him too.

Hotel de la Californie,
Rue Charlamagne,
Alger.
Monday.

Dear Madame Rana,

I have written to Mr. Rana why I do not come to see you before going. My sad heart clings to you and Mr. Rana and Perrin and our dear Ranjit, and if I come perhaps I shall wish to remain with you instead of parting again. For already this separation has given me much pain. Oh you cannot imagine it. So I do not wish to undergo the trial. Pray write to me sweetly, lovingly, so that I may feel that in some way your motherly care and protection are still with me. Think of me often, and give me your blessing now so that I may succeed in my work. You have saved my life by putting your own in danger, and so you should always think that I am.

Your own grateful but neughty boy,
Har Dayal.

Hotel de la Californie,
Rue Charlemagne,
Alger.
Tuesday, 8 a. m.

Dear Mr. Rana,

My letters must have convinced you that may departure is not the result of caprice nor is it due to the fact that "Indians have no application" as you complained one day. At least I am not one of those Indians. Nothing less than stern necessity would have induced me to travel like this in my present state of health. Nothing less than the call of Duty could have induced me to quit the haven of refuge in Paris for the dark stormy seas which lie before me. Nothing less would have led me to leave The Bande Mataram in other hands and interrupt my studies. Many books which I brought are lying unread in my bag ! And all chances of French conversation are over !

If I stay in Paris as I have been doing, I shall die soon. already the burden on the heart, due to the feeling that I was perhaps troubling others, was great, and gave me much continual worry. But now it is not physically possible for me to live like that. How can you blame me then ? Do you wish that I should die ? It is a physical impossibility now. So you will see that I am right. And surely you don't desire that I should pine away and die or go mad.

The other alternative I shall never adopt. No, never. All that for which I have struggled will be laid in the dust. And what have I ? I cannot endanger my yellow turban permanently like that. For fifteen months I have put it by for the sake of health. But to adopt this alternative would be to proclaim that I willingly renounce it for ever. No—no. Other men have things to console them. If one loses his mother he may have his wife to console him : if he loses one brother, he may find comfort in his son or another brother : if he loses some money, he has more in the bank : if he loses his wife, he has his children to love. But me, I have only this yellow rag in place of mother and brother and wife and child and wealth and rank and everything. That is the price I had paid for it. No, I shall now give it up. And for what? For mere food to eat and rags to wear, merely to live or be healthy. No—It is not worthwhile. I shall not barter it for a kingdom, not to speak of two meals a day and a bed at night. You perhaps think I am queer. Mr. Rana. But you can understand my ideas. I will fly to the remotest regions of the globe rather than permanently forfeit my right to the yellow turban. It is not essential for me to live in any particular place: but it is essential not to lose my whole fortune. Considerations of health induced me to put it aside for a time and adopt a regular and even bohemian life and to beg, fixed money contributions of my friends. Now I don't care for health : at any rate, I do not attach great importance to it. So I resume my turban and all that it stands for. It is the only thing that I possess in the world—it is my wealth and family and joy and everything. So do not think that I go in a fit of childish caprice. No. I see that things are at stake. I know my mind clearly. And I shall run all risks of ill-health, loneliness, fatigue, even a premature end for my object.

So pardon me for not coming in response to your call of love. There is a greater voice calling me away—that of my Master. I cannot disobey it.

Yours affectionately,
Har Dayal.

I send you some papers belonging to my Text Book of Politics about which I wrote to you. I brought them here for The Bande Mataram articles. Please put them in the manuscripts.

Already I had fever for a week after my arrival here. And my sleep and appetite are getting worse. But I shall run all risks.

Hotel de la Californie,
Alger.
Wednesday. 9 a. m.

Dear Mr. Rana,

I hear that Aiyar has bravely resigned his membership of the Bar. I think he intends to live outside India. Now if you can secure him for The Bande Mataram (failing Chatto), that will be all right. He can also write well. For example, if you pay him something and also help him to start in life like Govind, he might stay in Paris. This is only a suggestion. You can think over the matter.

My last letter has shown you that I don't go away from anger, caprice or anything of the kind, but from foresight and deliberation. Much is at stake ! All earnest youths of Northern India are watching me. They have known all my ideas and action. And now if I begin moneymaking, they will say, "He was all for living our professions when he was in India, but Europe spoiled him. He settled down to money making life in Paris. He began to take money for his articles and books ! What will those people say who have spent hundreds of rupees (big sums in India) at my slightest desire for my pupils and for my journey to Europe and during my illness simply on account of their knowledge of the fact that I was debarred from making money ? They will be disappointed, shocked. They will say, "His zeal lasted only one year. Europe spoiled him. He became avaricious and mercenary there. It happens like that with many men !" Their faith in me, based on their conviction that I have bidden gooobye, to all trades, professions and avenues of money-earning for ever will be lost ! And a great demoralisation will fall on earnest youths in the Punjab, who have still their eyes fixed on me. Some of them ask me that they like to see me if I pass near India anywhere in going to Japan !

And if I had become really mercenary in spirit, if I really desired money of my own, then I may fall, and that would be a calamity. That's all. But I do do not find any such desire in my heart. Lord Buddha guards me every moment. For one year I have troubled others by taking the initiative in begging regular money help, because the doctor told me that I must have proper food and rest. Now proper feeding was possible only in a home or in a pension (or under the land-lady system in England). Before I fell ill, my habits were undermining my health. The doctor told me that I should look to my health immediately. And so I had to suffer all that humiliation of Shyamaji affair. O God, what humiliation ! How my heart bleeds when I think of the affair ! How I was tempted to give up the method of not earning money for ever, for at Oxford I could then easily earn even £ 150 a year by work as a teacher for only one hour a day (tuition being paid at eight shillings six pence an hour there). That was really a sore trial. But now I find that the desire of restoring my nervous system to the normal condition in which it was during my days of good health has led to needless trouble for friends, and to the diversion of the "party" funds from other more useful purposes. I never wish to make my health a stumbling block in the way of "the party". No, never. At the same time, I shall not betray the trust reposed in me by all those who know my idealism. What will Chandu Lal and Jaswant Rai and others say who have faith in me absolutely ? And as I said. I do not find any desire for personal property, for a "bourse" of my own, in my heart. Then why fall ?

It is living in Europe and the desire of health that have caused the trouble to friends. Not so much living in Europe. for I lived at Oxford and in London six months without causing trouble to anybody. So now I leave this blessed constitution to take care of itself. I will care for my health of course. But I shall not go out of my way to trouble friends for money for my proper feeding or shelter or medicine or clothing. I shall take life as it comes—the true principle. And let health and strength come as they will. If they don't come so much the better.

You may not agree with my plans. You may think, with some one else, that "a man who is not himself independent cannot make India Independent." You may believe that "it is man's first duty to make himself self-supporting." You may think that it is better to live like Comte and Herbert Spencer and John Stuart Mill and have health and strength. But I have made the foundations of my life already. It is too late to change them for worse now. Hardships and fatigue and worry—all this is natural for a life like this, but I was prepared for all that when I left all channels of moneymaking and the protection of my home. I did not think that my method of work would make life a bed of roses for me.

I can of course fall and earn much money by journalism (like Saint Nihal Singh) and tuition (like the Berlin gentlemen you spoke of), but it is not for this lamentable conclusion that I have been toiling and moiling for years. To earn my yellow turban in India by leaving family and my social duties in abandoning my wife and child to live as beggars on the charity of my brothers, and by shutting out all avenues of money-earning, and to lose it in Europe for two meals a day and a bed at night ! No—No. My work will be ruined. I shall never do any good then. I shall go where I can get these two meals and that bed without selling my yellow turban for them and demoralising all my young comrades and all my comrades Northern India. To come from India a Sannyasi and to degenerate into a mercenary teacher or journalist! No—No. And for what ? Merely to live on, to keep body and soul together. It is a wretched law of nature that the body must be fed and that food is an economic affair! My heart has not become mercenary. And I shall not become mercenary in occupation merely to live in Europe or to be healthy and strong.

So, my dear Mr. Rana, don't be grieved that I go. Much good will come out of it. I never intended to explain the matter at great length or to pour out my heart before you as I have done in previous letters. But as I felt a heavy burden at my heart and felt inclined to cry every moment. I sought relief in telling you all my "chagrins" and also to account for a certain harshness that you may have noticed in my demeanour during the last days in Paris and to beg pardon for it. And I have explained all that is at stake in order to console you for my going and to convince you that I should go. You have claims upon me, and I cannot put off with a curt, brusque reply. Of course, I am not bound to explain my motives to everybody. But to you I owe a duty. So I have explained all.

I was horribly tempted to fall and become mercenary in occupation for the sake of living in Paris and studying at the University and regaining my strength by a quiet regular life. I was inclined to do it. But as I thought and thought, I discovered that it was not necessary to fall, if I could only give myself the trouble of journeying and leading an irregular life of some hardship and uncertainty. So I chose to face this rather than yield to seductions of a quiet and regular life and the opportunities of study and agreeable company and improvement in health and strength. Temptations come under various forms, but he who remains steadfast till the end conquers.

About Ranji, you should (as you agree already) ground him first in moral ideas before teaching him Indian politics and "patriotism", for he may think that a windbag kind of patriotism and hatred of England are the greatest virtues and make up for lack of simplicity truthfulness, honesty, etc., etc. Don't swell his mind with hatred of England and this windbag bluffy kind of "patriotism" first. It can come afterwards. The natural order is Morality first, then Politics and Patriotism. For morality comprises everything—patriotism is only a derived virtue and applies only to affairs relating to the State as against the States. If we had only one State in all the world, in which all were citizens, patriotism (as understood now) will not be a virture at all.

I shall write more later on.

Ever yours lovingly,
Har Dayal.

Hotel de la Californie,
Alger.
May 21, 1910.

Dear Madame Rana,

I was extremely happy to hear from you and dear Ranji. Our letters crossed.

I regret I am leaving for Japan via America next month according to my original plan, as this place is useless from all points of view. The public library of which I had read in a guide to Alger, is a wretched collection of old books, and I cannot carry on my studies here. Nor can I influence others, as there is no Indian community resident here. It is sheer waste of life to remain in this wilderness. So I leave next month on the 10th. If Paris lies on my route to America, I shall have the great pleasure to see you and Mr. Rana and Ranji and Perrin and other friends once more. For I don't know when we can see one another again in this life. On the contrary, if I don't pass through Paris on my way to America, I shall send you my sad au revoir from here.

I do request you to write to me wherever I am in this world. When I am no longer in this world, we shall see what we can do. But please consider it your duty to write to me. And let Ranji write to me also regularly. It gives me great delight to hear from him.

I am doing well, though I feel awfully lonely. Several days pass without my speaking to anyone I thus find more time for reflection and self-examination. Solitude is not a good companion, as Dr. Femet said, but it is sometimes good for moral health.

I have written to Mr. Govind to open my bags and send me some things which I shall want on my voyage. For I think I shall not be able to pass through Paris on my journey to America. And besides, a second meeting will be followed by a second parting! So the joy will be balanced by the pain. And I am already too much excited and saddended. So Mr. Govind will find out the things and he will pack them. I do not wish that you should take any trouble in this matter, as my big bag is full of all sort of rubbish. The small bag you can open yourself, if you like. Everything in it is quite "convenable".

I was reading the other day the following sentence on page 222 of the Gospel of Buddha :

"Has not the Blessed One formerly declared this to us, that it is in the very nature of all things near and dear unto us, that we must separate from them and leave them ?"

How is little Perrin doing ? Does she take some lessons at your place ? How I recall the pleasant afternoons that I have spent at your house on the occasion of those lessons! After all, memory is a boon, for we can think of the past and find pleasure in it.

Please convey my compliments to Madame Bottou and Mlle Bottou when they come to see you, and kiss little Jeanette for me. I was sorry I could not see her during my stay in Paris this time.

You should look well after Ranji, for a young man's character is formed between the age of 15 and 20. You should teach him to be simple. Don't let him become careful about dress. That is the first point. The danger is great in the atmosphere of French society in particular. And never let him use perfume, or silk handkerchiefs or silk socks or fashionable ties, or anything of the sort. Never let him waste time on arranging his hair beautifully will care. Spartan simplicity should be enforced in youth, so that the character should be manly and not "amolli". And the evil begins with dress, for a young man likes to be a beau.

Further, when he is little older, don't take him into society where he should meet girls—parties etc. For between the age of 17 and 22, much intercouse with girls should be avoided. It makes a man frivolous and produces the feeling of love precociously and distracts his attention from studies and moral ideas.

Further, from now banish all novels and dramas from his studies. No novel, no drama. After 22, he can read them. For novels and dramas corrupt the mind at this age. The books to be read at this age should be the following—

Books of adventure and travel.

Biographies of Great Men.

Books of Natural History and Science written in a popular form for boys.

Books of Morals.

Histories written in a popular style.

Descriptions of different countries.

On the contrary, novels and dramas give no useful information, while they corrupt the mind.

For a man's character—his "penchant"—is formed between 15 and 22. He can become serious and earnest or frivolous and lax during these years. And the books that we read in youth influence our character immensely.

I shall write more later on.

It has been raining all day to-day.

I shall begin to learn your German in 2 or 3 months. Next year I shall write to you in German. Then perhaps you will reply sooner!

I am always thinking of the pleasant days that I spent in Paris in the company of loving friends and comrades. An oasis in the midst of the desert of a philosopher's life.

With best wishes,

Yours sincerely,
Har Dayal.

P. S. I am sorry I shall not pass through Paris on my way to America. The boat leaves on the 10th (June).

Hotel de la Calafornie,
Alger.

Dear Ranji,

I was very glad to hear from you. You should always write to me. You write very good English. Tell me what books you are reading these days. How is your bicycle going on ?

I shall send you other books from time to time. I am going to Japan next month via America. I shall write to you about everything that I see there.

With much love,

Yours affectionately,
Har Dayal.

Poste Restante,
Alger.
May 14, 1910.

Dear Mr. Rana,

I have not heard from you lately. I am so lonely here that a few days seem like ages. The other day I was extremely happy to hear from Madame Rana.

I regret I have to revert to my first idea of going to Japan, as there is nothing to do in this place. The Bibliotheque, of which I had read in a book on Algerie, is only a small collection of old books and is worthless. The "Universite" is only a sort of school for Arabs. That is all. It is only a commercial place and there is no opportunity of any work. So I can neither carry on my studies here nor influence others. It is sheer waste of life, rotting in this wilderness.

About The Bande Mataram, I have asked Madame Cama and Mr. Aiyar to ask Chattopadhyaya to undertake it. He will agree that the continuance of the journal is necessary, as it is a useful institution of the party. He wields a facile pen : so four pages a month will not be any trouble to him. Rather he should be glad to do the duty. I have not written to him directly as I don't know him well at all. He is Mr. Aiyar's friend and Mr. Aiyar can arrange the matter easily.

There is no need of my expressing any regret for this, as you know how I have been pained and upset to leave Paris and my friends and my studies and literary work to go wandering like this in search of a place where to live. Well, it is all over, and I shall try to do whatever I can, wherever I find myself.

The boat leaves on the 10th June. I shall send the MSS, for the July number (of The Bande Mataram) before my departure,

How is everybody getting on ?

I shall stay a short time in New York.

Yours affectionately,
Har Dayal.

You can also write to Mr. Chattopadhyaya if you know him.

Kindly give the other slips to Jayaswal and Mme Rana and to Mr. Govind.

Please ask Mr. Govind to send my things as soon as possible, by return of mail, as I may leave this hotel afterwards. It is necessary that I should get them soon.

Alger.
Monday.

Dear Mr. Rana,

I have already written about The Bande Mataram. Most probably I shall not reach Japan but remain in or near the United States. So I shall be able to go on with the little good work that I am able to do in carrying on The Bande Mataram. So don't be anxious now. I did not imagine that Chattopadhyaya was not free.

I shall send you the MSS. for the July and August numbers before departure. So there will be no delay. Then I shall send the MSS. for September from America.

Please do not send anything for me to New York as I shall sail not for New York but La Havana (Cuba).

Do not be sad that I go. It is necessary for my peace of mind, for my future career, and for the Interests of my comrades and co-workers. I know it is necessary. So don't worry. I shall take care of myself and I have a small sum of money with me for immediate necessities, which I have now reduced to the minimum possible. I shall write to you before sailing.

You have my article on "Education" for emergency purposes.

I did not think that Chattopadhyaya had no time even for The Talvar. I thought The Talvar was irregular for financial reasons. But now that I know the truth. I shall try my utmost to keep up The Bande Mataram consistently with my other duties. If I remain in or near the United States (as is possible), there will be no difficulty whatever. And in that case, I may hope to see you again some time.

I sail from Bordeaux on the 23rd for La Havana (Cuba). I shall write to you from Bordeaux.

Fondest love to Ranji.

Aiyar has asked me to edit The Talvar too. I don't know what to say. Who pays for the printing? Are the financial arrangements for printing satisfactory?

Yours affectionately,
H. D.

Please give the other letter to Govindaji without delay. I want some books, as the voyage will take three weeks, and I should have something to read both to occupy myself and not to waste time.

I leave Alger on the 18th and sail from Bordeaux on the 23rd

San Francisco.
September 14, 1913.

Dear Hanwant Sahaiji,

It is my intention that you should start from there in the month of March and come here, because it is necessary that you should come out (of India). . . . You should continue the study of the French language. It is very necessary.

I shall send you full instructions for coming here but not now. You should remind me about the month of March. I shall send all directions. You should not come by way or New York. It will cost you much. Rupees six hundred will suffice for coming via San Francisco.

I will issue one Urdu and one Gurmukhi weekly paper from this place. The men of this place have collected money. There are many Hindus here. You should write to me the addresses to which this newspaper is to be sent. I shall not send it at all to the addresses of your other "friends."

Yours sincerely,
Har Dayal

Molnlycke.
November 25, 1922.

My dear Professor Arne,

Now I have definitely decided to settle down in Sweden. I intend to go to Uppsala next year. I hope to begin with my philosophical publications in two or three years.

I wish to become a member of the Oriental Society in Stockholm. Please let me know the annual subscription (if there is no objection). Who is the head of the institution?

In December I will present my application for citizenship. I should be very grateful if you personally speak to the Minister of Justice in order to recommend me. Naturally I shall have many good references from eminent Swedes belonging to all political parties (even from the right). I have finished "political" activity of all kinds, as I think I must devote myself to popular ethical and intellectual education.

Must I can myself "Dayalson" when I become a Swede? I am just studying Swedish poetry.

Yours affectionately,
Har Dayal.

Molnlycke.
February 26, 1923.

My dear Professor Arne,

I sent an article to the newspaper Dagens Nyketer in Stockholm. You have helped me in getting it published. I, therefore, thank you. I will now move to Stockholm and finish with the wandering life, even if I do not get citizenship. I have sent to the Swedish Government my application along with two papers showing that I am a member of scientific societies in France and England which signifies that the last-named country has nothing against my personal political standpoint. The papers could be shown to lector E. Wigforss.

Yours affectionately,
Har Dayal.

Molnlycke.
April 13, 1923.

My dear Professor Arne,

The resignation of the Government complicates my case. I must try to do all that is possible with the new Minister of Justice.

I hope we shall get a liberal government. If not, I probably have to wait for the next socialistic government which will come after the elections in 1925. Up to that date I will serve as a teacher at the "People's High School". In this respect it is a good position for the next application in 1925. I think the gentlemen of the right party will do away with unnecessary difficulties.

From other points of view I am glad that the government has resigned. Then I think that a socialistic government would depend upon a majority in the Parliament.

I hope to see you in Goteburg in July.

Yours affectionately,
Har Dayal.

Molnlycke (Sweden).
12th Dec., '23.

Dear Swami Satya Devaji,

Thanks for your kind letter. I shall reply to your questions in order.

1. I do not wish to work with the revolutionary Indian nationalists of Berlin and California. I do not think they can accomplish anything. I approve of the Home Rule Party which aims at Self-Government for India within the British Empire, like Ireland. I have set forth my attitude in full in some articles written in 1919.

2. Within the Home Rule Party I work only for the poor classes, the farmers and the labourers. I do not wish to work for or with rich men—landlords, lawyers, capitalists, etc. Why should one make sacrifices for the sake of these rich classes? They plunder the people. I am a Socialist and I have written several letters to The Labour Leader of London from the standpoint of an Indian Socialist and Home Ruler.

3. I devoted myself to Indian movements fifteen years ago, and sacrificed everything for them. But what has been the result? Only sickness and waste of time and energy. Is it not so? Well, why do you advise me to begin again? The

students and the common people of India can show much zeal and courage, but your rich men will never give money for any movement. They love money more than anything else in the world. And what can your educated men do without money, especially when they wish to organise political movements? Thus all your sacrifice will be useless and fruitless, as you will never get money from the rich people. This has been my experience. No one helped me with money when I was ill in foreign countries, and nothing could be done for the movement.

4. I have not married in Sweden. I am already married in India, and my wife and daughter are in Delhi. I hear from them regularly and they may come to Sweden, if circumstances permit.

5. I have no passport of any kind, not even a British passport. How can I travel? Further, no amnesty has been declared in India, and I have already been condemned by the law-court there for many political offences. So I must live here as a refugee.

6. I am willing to write good books in Hindi and Urdu for the people of India. You have so much noise and agitation in India, but you have very few good books on history, politics, modern civilisation etc. Such books are necessary, for the enlightenment of the public, and many useful movements will arise on the soil thus prepared. I give much time to study and shall be glad to initiate a series of good books of this kind. Here in, Europe, the public mind is first trained and elevated by many such books, which are sold at a cheap price. If you can help me in this plan I shall be thankful. It is an important plan.

If you pass Gothenburg at any time, I shall be happy to see you. Please inform me if you happen to travel by this route. I must give a course of lessons at a school next week. I earn my living in this country by giving lessons and lectures in Swedish so it is impossible for me to come to Stockholm.

Please write to me if you can arrange for the publication of books in Hindi and Urdu. The real Renaissance in India requires a large number of good books translated or compiled from different European languages. Don't you think so?

With best wishes,

Yours sincerely,
Har Dayal.

Molnlycke (Sweden).
(?) Dec., '23.

Dear Swami Satya Devji,

I have written to you about a practical plan. I wish to write several books in Hindi and Urdu during the next few years, dealing with democratic movements in Europe and America, the lives of great leaders, etc. I also wish to translate some great European books on Politics and Sociology into Hindi and Urdu. In this way I can give India all that I have learnt and acquired through my studies. The foundations of future democratic movement in India will thus be laid firm and deep. Such books are absolutely necessary.

If you know some nationalists, who can spend money on this plan, you can write to me. The Indian 'Patriots' have plenty of money, but I have lived on the chatity of foreign friends and acquaintances. This is not very encouraging. Many people talked of my 'sacrifice' and 'personality', but no one helped me with money for my work or even for my personal need in foreign countries! Such are your rich 'nationalists' in India. Nothing can be done under such circumstances. Why do you blame me? I wished to write these books in 1909, but there was no money for the work.

You can arrange for the publication of the books in India. I leave it entirely to you and your friends. There is no danger in co-operating with me now, as I am not a 'revolutionary' politician now, and this is only literary work of an educational tendency. I correspond with my friends in England and India, and I am a member of scientific societies in England. You can safely carry out this plan, if you like.

Well, you should reply to this letter and not blame me for inactivity. I can do this important work here during the next few years, if your nationalist friends can help me with money. If they cannot do so, let the matter drop. But don't blame me in future. I cannot do impossible things. Let the Indian 'Patriots' perish with their money.

Through these books entire history and spirit of European Democracy and Freedom can be transferred to Hindi and Urdu, and this is the real fundamental work. It will bear fruits during the whole of the twentieth century.

Now it is for you to think over the matter.

Some time in the future, I may come to India and take part in the practical work of political organisation. But at present, I must write these books, if the nationalists can help with money.

I shall call the whole series Rajaniti-Shastra or Rajanaiti-Darshan. Such a political shastra will produce many patriots, democrats, social reformers and idealists during the next fifty years.

With best wishes,

Yours sincerely,
Har Dayal.

Molnlycke (Sweden).
25.1.24.

Dear Swami Satya Devaji,

I am very happy to learn that you are willing to help me to publish these books. I wished to stay in London and write this series in 1909 and the following years, and appealed to our nationalist friends and 'leaders' to try and arrange for my residence in London. I was only a young man then. But it was not found possible to get together the small amount of money needed for the whole plan! So I had to travel about aimlessly in America and Europe. That was when you met me in Boston. I was practically doing nothing for India then. It was sheer waste of life after so much aspiration and sacrifice. I did not complain in my letters about recent events that have happened since 1918. I referred to the failure of these plans in 1909 on account of want of money. I regard these books as my best gift to our people. I believe in the great influence and power of such books among young men next to the inspiring effect of personal sacrifice. When I finish this series, I shall feel as if I had repaid a rin (debt) to India. The next fifty years will show the awakening power of this series. We want a general all-round "Renaissance" in India (especially in India states) and not merely this or that particular social or political movement with its limited programme. Of course our activity must run in these different channels and new parties, organisations, samajas and movements with special aims must arise. But we want first to transplant all the ideas and ideals of Europe and America to the Indian languages. I do not much believe in the popular influence of books and newspapers written in English. Even B.A.'s and M.A.'s enjoy and understand new ideas better in their matri-bhasha (Mothertongue). When we have put everything that is lofty and inspiring in European culture and history before our countrymen in a systematic and thorough manner, we have discharged a great duty as 'educated' Indians. This is the seed that must be sown.

I shall begin today to prepare the first volume of the series. I travel about in villages and towns during the winter. I can send you only one book very soon as I shall have to write and translate at hotels, while I am travelling and lecturing. But I shall be free from this work in April, and then I shall be able to write more quickly in summer. Some books will consist only of translations of standard historical books which have been translated into all modern languages, and which every civilized nation should possess in its own tongue. Other books will be written by me on different subjects. You can find a name for the whole series, such as Europiya Granthamala. Navin Sabhyata Prakashini or Western Civilization Series, etc. The volumes on Rajaniti Vijnan (political science) will be a part of it, dealing with politics and freedom. But many other subjects will come in. Many great well-known books will be translated from Greek, Latin, French, German, Italian and English. I hope that other active educated men will join in the work later on.

To begin with I send you a Hindi translation of an old Greek book, Diogenes Lucretius' Lives of Great Philosophers. It is also desirable that I should not begin at once with a very political book, as I wish to create a general 'Renaissance' Spirit, and not to do any political agitation directly or indirectly. The entire national life must be raised to a higher plane.

I shall first write about ancient Greece and its history, etc. That is the first important thing for all Asiatic nations. You know that modern European civilization is based on Greek ideals. In fact, the study of Greek books started the modern movement in Italy in the 15th century and freed Europe from the mystics, priests, monks and ascetics of the middle ages. That is what has made Europe great and democratic. So I regard it as my first task to transfer to Hindi as much as possible about Greece. These will be the first volumes. As they all deal with ancient civilization, they will only help general culture and cannot be regarded as 'political books'. You see many Indians are so timid that I have to reassure them now. I know their psychology.

I wish that you would kindly consider the following points :

1. The books should also be translated there in simple Urdu and Punjabi.

2. Please make special arrangements for the sale of the books in the Indian States. Kindly send some agents to arrange for the sale through book-sellers or newspaper offices in Patiala, Indore, Srinagar and other towns in the States. Better

movements will arise in the half-free states than in enslaved British India.

3. If binding does not raise the prices too much please sell them bound in cloth, or both in cloth, and paper.

4. The price should be low so that shop-keepers, farmers and students can buy them. I myself do not wish to receive any money for them. So you can publish them for the common people, not for the "educated" lawyers. I wish to reach the students and the farmers, and these classes cannot buy a book worth more than annas twelve or one rupee. If necessary, a big book may be published in two parts but each separate volume must be small and cheap. It is necessary to think of our public. In no case must the price exceed rupee one. The average price should be annas eight. The size of the volume can be reduced, if necessary.

More again.

Please buy for me and send me the best and biggest English-Hindi Dictionary that you can get there. I shall need such a dictionary to find new Hindi terms for various English words. I have not read any Hindi book or paper for six years, as I thought that I had cut off all connections with India and Indian movements. Please also send me some books of new Hindi poetry. I want an English-Hindi dictionary, not a Hindi-English dictionary.

With love,

Yours sincerely,
Har Dayal.

Stockholm (Sweden).

Dear Satya Devaji,

I am so glad to receive your letter. I introduce you to a wonderful man. He met me here. This gentlemen says that his name is "Garlic King". He gave me some recipes which have done me good. I am confident that you too would be glad to meet him. He meets you soon in Bieden. Kindly give him a patient hearing.

Yours sincerely,
Har Dayal.

Appelviken (Sweden).
January 18, 1925.

Dear friend Shri Narayan Prasadji,

Please accept my love and salutation.

I am pleased to read the book you have sent me. Your translation is very good. I think you for this.

Now I will write in Hindi and Urdu. If for other provinces I have to write in English I will translate from Hindi and get it published. Mother tongue should be the main language. In 1908 I had not pondered over this question.

I have sent an article, 'The way to Swarajya' to Pranvir. You examine it critically. There are new ideas therein.

I am quite fit. It is very cold here.

Yours faithfully,
Har Dayal.

Appelviken (Sweden),
April 8, 1925.

Dear Panditji.

Please accept my salutation.

I am very grateful to you for sending me a copy of your Bihari Satsai. It is very kind of you. I read this before, when I was in Germany. But there was no commentary. I, therefore, could not understand it thoroughly. With the help of your commentary it should be easy. Your comparative criticism is praiseworthy. Hindi literature needs this very badly. I have been able to enjoy your book and it will ever be a source of enjoyment. I am a lover of poetry.

Kindly write to me if I could be of any service while I am in Europe.

Yours sincerely,
Har Dayal.

Molnycke (Sweden).
8.7.25.

My dear Raghubar Dayal.

Thanks for your kind letter. Kishan dada said it was better to put off the plan of buying a cottage. Perhaps I can get an amnesty, but it is very doubtful. At present, it is best to stay at Molnlycke.

I am rather diffident in suggesting a course of study for your energetic friend, but I think that the following books will be useful :

*Bryce—Modern Democracies
*Wells—History of Mankind
*Van Loon—History of Mankind
*Livingstone—The Legacy of Greece
*Aristotle—Nicomachean Ethics
*Xenophon—Memorabilien
*Plato—The Republic
*Plato—The Socratic Dialogues
*Plutarch—Lives of Greeks And Romans
*Diogenes Laertius—Lives of Greek Philosophers
*Paul Carus—Gospel of Buddha
Renan—Life of Christ
Mohamed Ali—Mohamed the Prophet
*Legge—Life and Works of Confucius
Legge—Life and Works of Mencius
*Gould—Concise History of Religion
*Robertson—Short History of Freethought
Frederic Harrison—Positivist Calendar

*Stone—The History of Labour
*Fisher—The Republican Tradition in Europe
Carlyle—The French Revolution
*Kropotkin—The Great Revolution
Morse—Stephens—Orators of the French Revolution
*Mary Wollstonecraft—Vindication of the Rights of Woman
*J. S. Mill—Subjection of Women
J. S. Mill—Utilitarianism
*Herbert Spencer—Education
*S.Coit—Message of Man
Science Histories—Series published by Watts & Co
*Life—Stories of Famous Men-Series published by Watts & Co
*Bluntschli—Theory of the State
*Locke—On Civil Government
*Rousseau—The Social Contract
*Marx—The Communist Manifesto
Haeckel—The Riddle of the Universe
Hyndman—Awakening of Asia
Caffin—How to Study Architecture
*Whitcomb—Young People's Story of Art
Flower—A History of Sculpture
*The Statesman's Year-Book
Dowden—Primer of Shakespeare

I think that this list will suffice. I have not included books on India, as these are well-known and can be easily purchased in India through Messrs, Natesan & Co., Madras. An all-round liberal education should be aimed at. But much depends on the method of study and the intellectual capacity of the person.

Very important books are marked with '*' in the list.

I shall always be glad to suggest books for the study of any special subject.

Please excuse the delay in replying to your letter, as I have not had much peace of mind lately. I have asked dear Bhagwat to come here in September.

With much love,

Your affectionate uncle & friend,
Har Dayal.

P.S. I am very happy to learn of the brilliant success achieved by dear Goghe. I hope she will have a College education. I am writing for 'The People', edited by Lala Lajpat Rai. My first Hindi book will deal with the life of Montesquieu, Professor Malte Jacobson, who showed you the big school building at Gothenburg, is now in England. His address is : Drayton Hall, West Drayton (Middlesex).

Molnlycke (Sweden).
29.7.1925.

My dear Raghubar Dayal,

Thanks for your kind letter. I am all right now, but I am back again in the old room with all the disorder and discomfort. During the hot weather, the milk has not been good, and that caused some trouble in the stomach. But I went on a short change of diet, and I am working on my Hindi book again.

Glad to get the 'Bharat'. It is very interesting. I am glad that you met Prof. Jacobson in London. He is a very kind man.

Please tell Bhagwat that he should come to me in December and spend the Christmas vacation with me. I have received an invitation to travel north in September and deliver some lectures. So I shall not be at home in September. Please write to him immediately. I have also written to him c/o Cook. It is best that he should come during the Christmas Holidays. Tell him that it is not very cold at Gothenburg. That is a wrong idea in foreign countries. The western coast of Sweden is not cold at all. It is like England.

Mr. and Mrs. Aurell and Ingrid, send you their best greetings.

With much love,

Yours affectionately,
Har Dayal.

2

Social Ideology

Education has been defined as a process of training and development that enables individuals or nations to make the best use of the faculties with which they have been endowed. The individual cannot work out his moral, intellectual and physical growth unless he profits by the accumulated experience and wisdom of generations gone by, and the nation is prevented from attaining its full stature and realising its destiny in the scheme of the Universe, if the individuals composing it are denied the opportunity of developing their gifts and capacities according to the most efficient methods known to the age when they happen to be born.

But man cannot live and grow alone. He is a gregarious animal. He is meant to be social and sociable. He who loves solitude, it has been wisely remarked, is either a God or a beast. Human nature is so constituted that men have always found delight and satisfaction in association as a primary condition of their welfare. Isolate a man from his fellow-beings, shut him up in a secluded corner away from the haunts of men, and he will dwindle and decay till all that is best in him, his intellect and impulse, his social instincts, and his moral nature, perishes so utterly that he is reduced to the level of a brute.

Association brings home to a man the duties that he owes to others, and thus supplies the one condition essential to moral development. For him who comes into real contact with all types and ranks of men, human brotherhood remains no empty phrase, but becomes a living creed ennobling and elevating his every day conduct. Thus the first object of education ought to be to impress on the mind of every child the sanctity of his duty to humanity which may be translated into theological language as his duty towards God. As the soul is the immortal part of man, as morality takes precedence of the intellect in all systems of conduct, we must place the gradual evolution of the sense of duty to mankind as the primary object of a healthy educational system. If this result is secured, the race will produce many noble men, whose names are cherished by millions after them; but if this ethical aspect to education is ignored, the nation will give birth to moral and intellectual pygmies, contemptible creatures whose lives are short, miserable and brutish. Thus does Dharma protect a race which keeps it alive, as the ancient Rishis declared. But this great Dharma of universal charity and goodwill, this ideal of Ahimsa, cannot be realised by an individual, unless he first establishes particular relations with the smaller social unit of which he forms a part. A long process of historical evolution has resulted in the formation of well-defined, compact social groups, which are marked off from one another by distinct and unmistakable features relating to manners and customs, language and religion, history and social environment. These groups of men associated together in States, tribes, Jirgahs or clans, are called 'nations', and a nation is therefore that a portion of humanity in the midst of which an ordinary man lives, moves and has his being for all practical purposes of life. Before Steam and Electricity caused that shrinkage of the world which enables us to go round the globe in 80 days, these nations remained more or less isolated from one another, each following the path of development on which it had set out in the early portion of its history. The 19th century almost annihilated space, has brought the Briton next door to the Zulu and the Malay, and has lifted the veil from off the face of Tibet. Nothing is now inaccessible to man, except perhaps the South Pole. The doctrine of nationality has thus been brought to prominence as the chief factor in the struggle which has followed he increased opportunities for intercommunication.

God has so willed it that mankind should contribute to the advent of the "far off divine event to which the whole creation moves" by dividing themselves into large groups which possess different capabilities and aptitudes, and are bound together by special ties of blood and religion and common history. Unity in variety seems to be the law of human progress as revealed in the history of the world for the last 3,000 years. A man can fulfil his duty to humanity by trying to come into direct contact with his fellowmen at the antipodes and ministering to their wants, but in that case his life will bear no relation to his actual surroundings. He will waste his energies in running after a phantom, in building a superstructure without a foundation. A mere cosmopolitan may entertain noble aspirations, but he cannot embody his ideas in the present. All the institutions of a race depend for their vitality on a proper relation between the educational system and the facts of external life. A type of character which does not accord with the social environments or the institutions of the nation will be a cause of disintegration and disorganization. Harmony between the individual spirit and the social group which should lead the former to subordinate its selfish promptings to the good of the latter, is essential for national existence.

Having developed the national type of character and brought it into line with the national modes of life, education should direct the youth to activities which should afford him an opportunity of fulfilling his duty to the nation. Hence the choice of a profession, which confronts a man as the gravest of problems at the threshold of life. We regard a profession as the sphere of work in which a man fulfils his Dharma. A profession is not meant to enable one to carn a livelihood for one's selfish purposes. We reject without hesitation the individualistic theories of livelihood propounded by those who confound the man with the stomach. The necessity of earning a livelihood is patent. Says Herbert Spencer in his essay on education : "We need not insist on the value of that knowledge which aids in direct self-preservation by facilitating the gaining o1 a livelihood. This is admitted by all and indeed by the mass perhaps too exclusively regarded as the end of education.

The choice of a profession supplies a man with the material wealth without which national existence is impossible, or it enables him to render services to society which are indispensable for its welfare. Hence all professions in a healthy society may be divided into productive and non-productive: the former category including those callings which directly produce commodities for enjoyment, and the latter class comprising those avocations which do not directly help in the production of commodities, but which preserve the conditions necessary for the production of commodities. Persons who perform functions other than the production and transmission of wealth are allowed a share of the wealth produced by the community not as a personal reward for doing their duty, but as a means of enabling them to discharge that duty in the best possible manner. Hence it is a mistake to regard income and professions from a selfish point of view—everything must be subordinated to Dharma.

Hence we find that an ideal system of education should satisfy the following conditions:

(1) It must awaken in boys a sense of their duty to humanity and the nation;

(2) It must form the national type of character;

(3) It must accustom boys to the national modes of life and thought which are around them;

(4) It must make them fit for some form of activity, by which they should develop their nature and carry out their Dharma.

This form of activity is called a Profession and the allowance of material wealth accorded to the person by the Society is called his Income. Thus Livelihood follows tangible institutions without taking help from the living doctrine of Nationality. For it is so ordained that no one, not even a Tolstoy, shall establish direct relations with Humanity except through the transforming medium of National Sentiment. We may in our impatience find fault with this ordering of human events as the product of narrow minds and half-developed moral instincts. We may look upon the principle of nationality as a stumbling block in the way of the man who tries to rise to the full height of his nature. But there it is, the hard fact of life, which one can deny only at his peril—the deep, ineradicable, irresistible instinct that shattered the cunningly woven fabrics reared by the clever hands of a Joseph II and a Napoleon. You may as well deny the presence of family affection as a determining factor in social affairs. Indeed modern history resolves itself only into a record of the assertion by nationalities of their separate consciousness as against the encroachment of some 'Imperial' power.

The education, which aims at making a perfect man of the child who is born to-day, should enable the young boy to realize his duty to Society and Humanity in general; and for the effective discharge of that obligation it should teach him his responsibilities towards that portion of mankind in whose history and character he naturally participates, a nd among whom he will live and grow and form close and enduring relations extending to all activities that help to further his individual progress.

Thus is the Darmah of Ahinsa related to the Dharma of national existence as the abstract to the concrete, as the general to the particular, as the ideal to the actual.

Hence the Primary object of my well-devised sound system of education in a civilized country should be the awakening of a sense of duty to the nation as the largest practicable social unit towards which an average man can establish constant relations, and with regard to which he can assume definite responsibilities. What shall it profit a nation if it gain the whole world but lose its own soul, like ancient Rome in the later days of empire, like Ireland in the nineteenth century. Learning, wealth, culture, polished manners, art and science in their most beautiful forms,—all these will follow in due time of this essential requisite of individual and national growth is provided, viz., the Patriotism or espirit de corps which inspires those who realise their duty towards the nation.

How is this result to be brought about? What are the methods by which a community keeps alive the vital principle which alone can preserve it from decay? How is this Promethean spark to be kept up in successive generations like the never-to-be-extinguished Jyoti that lights up the shrine of Badrinath? For it cannot be asserted too often that a system of education which impairs or does not develop a sense of social duty is worse than useless, even though it should turn out intellectual prodigies and cover the face of the land with academies and institutes. Not by science alone does a nation live and thrive. No amount of booklore or scientific knowledge or oratorical gifts, no discoveries in the domain of science or archaeology, no laurels placed on the brows of savants by admiring nations, no literatures and philosophies can compensate a nation for the weakening, even in the slightest degree, of that social spitit which constitutes its vitality. How foolish would a people be who sold away their life for little learning? Learning is good, in its place, but the paramount aim of a healthy educational system is the formation and growth of that feeling of social solidarity which is at the basis of all progress.

Education must therefore begin with the history of the race to which the boy belongs. The individuality of a nation consists in the mass of tradition and historical memories which should form the intellectual equipment of even the meanest and the most uncultured member of the social group. This historical tradition distinguishes one nation from another—it is the chief badge of nationality, the sign of freemasonry that gives admission to its sacred circle. All that the race has done is its treasure, the deeds it had wrought, the thoughts it has perfected, the emotions it has felt, the arts it has developed, the revolutions it has undergone, all this and much more the race preserves and transmits from generation as an heirloom never to be cast aside. Thus the boy is made to feel that he is bound by indissoluble ties to those who have gone before him, that he as a part in all the experiences of his race and that he must merge his little life in the vaster and grander life of the nation. The awakening of patriotism through the teaching of national history is thus the first requisite of a sound educational system.

And this training resolves itself into several elements :

(1) The teaching of historical tradition.

(2) The consequent formation of a certain type of character, and

(3) The reproduction of the social environment of the nation in the life of the school, as the customs and manners of a people are the result of the process of historical growth it has passed through.

The formation of the national Type of character and the imparting of a love for the national manners and customs and modes of thought and life follow as corollaries from the duty of teaching of the national historical tradition. The past is brought home to the student as a means of enabling him to do his duty, a profession as a necessary consequence, but is not its main object. A man walking in the sun casts a shadow behind him, but no man walks in the sun for the express purpose of casting the shadow.

We shall in our next discuss the nature of the professions for which a healthy system of education should prepare the boys of a nation, and shall then apply the general principles elaborated above to test the effects of the educational system established in India on the nation's welfare and progress.

The choice of a profession with the object of fulfilling one's social Dharma is one of the most important duties in life. In fact nothing moulds a man's character and shapes his course of conduct more effectively than his profession. Some people would regard marriage as a more potent factor in the building up of individual character than profession. But this proposition is not unexceptionable. Let both "divide the crown". Certain it is that a man's wife and his calling exert the greatest influence on him, for better or for worse, throughout his worldly career. It, therefore, behoves us to exercise the utmost care and judgment in the selection of both of them. Let a man consider how he can best benefit his society and choose accordingly.

The choice of a profession with the help of advertisements in newspapers is apt to land an honest man in strange difficulties. But how few are those who deliberate about the right or wrong of the vocations which they desire to adopt, who take counsel with themselves as to whether they can conscientiously discharge the duties of the position they intend to take up! Livelihood for its own sake and at any cost seems to be the watchword of "educated" India at present. Bread and butter take precedence of Dharma. It is considered a sign of moral puritanism to discuss the moral aspects of any line of conduct that a man may adopt for the purpose of earning his living. This tone of national feeling betrays a sad decadence of the ethical standard of the nation. They who run only after bread shall lose it, but those who follow Dharma will obtain both Artha and Karma, as promised by the sage in Mahabharta. This, then, is the first test which must be applied to any profession—is it socially beneficial? Does it involve no serious breach of the moral law? A profession which raises an able man to the highest pinnacle of fame and glory, but undermines the vitality of the nation, stands self-condemned. I shall discuss the bearing of this great principle on the question of "Government Service", "the Bar" and other cognate topics.

Further, a profession must enable man to do the maximum good to his nation. It is not enough to persuade oneself that one is not inflicting any injury on humanity in general. It is necessary that every citizen should exert himself with all his might to make himself serviceable to the "State" which represents his community. A profession is one of the many paths to perfection which are open to him, and he should always consider himself responsible to the "State" for the use that he makes of his powers of mind and body. If a man endowed with uncommon intellectual gifts becomes a cobbler or a hawker, he is cheating humanity of its due. He is an unfaithful steward. His profession is only a negative form of theft.

Having indicated the general principles on which we must proceed in order to construct a healthy educational system for our boys, we should apply them to our present day problems. And there lies the rub. Most of t he truths outlined above are, people would say, mere truisms. Every school boy knows them, or at least ought to know them. Every president of a University Convocation dins these beautiful formulae into our ears. We are tired of them. Let us hear something new. Mark Twain at Geneva said to the guide who showed him an Egyptian mummy, "Sir, I have not travelled so far to see an old corpse." Even so our "educated" men may turn away in disgust from these old friends who are always reappearing with new faces.

I admit the justice of this complaint. But I desire to vary the theme. I do not wish to indulge in mere platitudes about educational ideas. I wish to apply them to existing conditions, a painful and arduous task. I shall now proceed to show how.

(i) the "educational" system established by the British Government in India is unsound, abnormal and pernicious in all its ramifications.

(ii) a national educational system can be evolved out of the material that at present is at our command.

Let us take up the work of destructive criticismfirst. The jungle must be cleared before we can make a road through it. The seif-complacency of the "educated" classes who are never weary of admiring one another as products of the "University System" must receive a shock before they can realize the aims and effects of English educational policy in India. Old gods must be dethroned. However painful the process may be, it must be done. I feel keenly on this point. British educational policy is killing out the soul of the nation.

The whole machinery of schools and colleges, 'normal' and 'abnormal', aided and unaided, Vernacular and Anglo-Vernacular, is one huge octopus which is sucking out the moral life-blood of the nation. It is crushing out the heart and conscience of our middle and upper classes. Our young men are slowly dying a death, far more dreadful than mere physical dissolution, infinitely more pitiable than the end of the crazy suicide—a death of all that is noble and praise-worthy in their character and habits, a social, moral and intelletual death which leads to no resurrection, either in this world or the next. This spectacle of a nation killing its Self, its Life without knowing it, moves me tears, Alas that it should be so !

I know there are persons, perfectly "honourable men", who look upon the British educational system as the panacea for our ills. For all purposes of social, political and religious reformation, they prescribe only one formula "Education". But they do not stop to inquire : "What sort of education !" They take it for granted that the educational facilities afforded by the British Government will lead to the progress of our nation. This belief is a sort of religion with them. It is heresy to dispute it. An Anglo-Vernacular High School is to them a temple : a College is airtha (holy place of pilgrimage). I shall dispose of their arguments after a discussion of the objects and the effects of the educational system established by astute and far-seeing foreigners in our country.

Nothing is more instructive than history. Let us see how and why the British Government established schools and colleges in India after the establishment of their dominion. There are two sides to this question.

Some people would have us believe that the rulers took pity on us. They saw on old and capable nation sunk in "superstition and ignorance." They came as representatives of a progressive civilization glorious in arts and arms. They desired to raise these poor, illiterate Hindus, "half devils, half children", to their own level.

They came as merchants and tax-gatherers; but as time passed they began to think of better things than gold. They wanted to make prayaschitta for all the sins of omission and commission committed by the pioneers of empire in Bengal and elsewhere. They therefore looked after our health, our education and our general welfare. Heavensent missionaries of culture and enlightenment, they have for more than 150 years laboured to impart European knowledge to a rude and untutored race. The British people deserve our heart-felt thanks for this great boon. The English education is a free gift from the Government to the people.

The Government may be, in some respects, as bad as some of its critics make out. It may be cruel, exacting, arbitrary, But no one can deny that it has proved its generosity by "educating" us, thus converting the old-fashioned, uncouth Pandits into wideawake "graduates" who are ever in touch with the latest developments of modern civilization. What a transformation ! Alas ! had the Gods churned the ocean a little longer, they would surely have found a fifteenth Ratna in the shape of "English education". What a pity that Narada was not born in this age of Universities ! Let us praise the Government that has made us men. Mr. Mehta has spoken times without number of the "priceless boon of education". Here, at last, after patient search, we have found one "blessing" of British Rule—a real, tangible, positive "blessing", visible to all and sundry. Let us hold it fast. It is our only hope.

Further the advocates of English educational policy contend that the British showed rare magnanimity in thus accepting us as pupils. Western education imparted in their schools will surely lead to our political enfranchisement. The British knew this full well; but they were inspired by a lofty sense of duty. They could not help doing their duty as rulers. It is in their blood. Duty, dominion and drink are their favourities. The early rulers of India realized that education would one day result in the political emancipation of the people. Yet they persevered. What a sight ! Here are a body of foreign conquerors who have acquired sovereignty over a large country after a hundred years' hard fighting. Their dead lie unburied by the Kaveri and the Sutlej; their blood has watered many a field of battle. And now they systematically set themselves to undo all their work, to pave the way for self—extinction, by imparting education to the conquered races. Bentinck and Canning laboriously reverse the process initiated by Clive and Warren Hastings.

The first Governors-General were of course mere adventurers; they thought only of taxes, But a generation of sympathetic, benevolent and far-sighted statesmen followed : Munro, Elphinstone, Bentinck, Macaulay. They consulted the welfare of the ruled. They establihsed Schools, Courts, Dispensaries, Post Offices. They undertook the work of "consolidation" and "improvement". Blessed be their names. Let them be added to the Hindu pantheon.

They were not blind. Macaulay's famous despatch mentions the possibility of the grant of "European institutions" to Indians as a consequence of education. Lord Ellenborough said to Dwarka Nath Tagore that education meant the end of British autocracy. Mr. Mehta is fond of relating how Elphinstone pointed to a heap of educational text-books and said to Gibbs, "But that is our high-road back to Europe". Such pathetic stories have been related by several politicians. The Anglo-Saxon race is convinced that if Empire and Duty can't go together, the former must be sacrificed. This spirit should entitle the British rulers of India to a heavenly shower of flowers (pushpa-varsha), the reward of great virtue in Hindu mythology. Macaulay, Ellenborough and Elphinstone have taken us into their confidence; they have shown us the workings of their innermost soul. Here is unimpeachable evidence.

I hope I have set forth the views of the apologists for English education fairly and impartially. The speeches and writings of popular "leaders" like Mr. Gokhale and others abound in passages extolling the merits of the British educational system and exhorting Indians to praise the Government for its beneficence.

In my next, I shall discuss the real objects of the Government in establishing the educational system in India, basing my remarks on evidence extracted from official or semi-official documents. The confessions of an official are always interesting reading. They may remind us of another book by Colonel Meadows Taylor that we read in our school days. But that is, of course, merely coincidence.

The enlightened politicians who teach us that the Government established schools and colleges for our benefit, have perhaps not read the history of India in the nineteenth century. It is a pity that they should spread such erroneous ideas without studying the records which tell of the motives that animated the British conquerors to undertake the difficult task of imparting education to their subjects. General principles of Sociology deduced from a critical study of the history of the world may also help us in gauging the ideas that underlie the educational system of the Government. There is nothing new under the sun. What has been, is and shall be for ever more.

The history of India in ancient times being enacted over again on the same soil and also in Africa in the twentieth century. The relations of conquering races to their subjects form a very interesting and important study. History teaches us certain laws of general application which have governed and regulated those relations. It should be our aim to discover these great truths, which are as precious as any spiritual treasures embedded in holy lore and to profit by them in our present condition. What the Upanishads are to the individual soul, History is to the collective organization called a Nation—it is the means of self-realization and emancipation.

The British established schools and colleges in India with the object of strengthening their hold over the country, of laying firm the foundation of their power, of consolidating their dominion so that the risks to which a foreign ruler is always exposed may be reduced to a minimum. Of course, if it is assumed that this result has brought India all good and no evil, then and only then can the educational system be regarded as a source of unalloyed bliss for the Indian people. Then it would be, like mercy, twice blessed—it blesses him that teaches and him that is taught. It would envelop both the rulers and the ruled in a halo of glory as a consequence of participation in a common enterprise which produces only beneficial results.

That the British rulers regarded their educational policy as a great instrument for the consolidation of their power is evident from the anticipations they entertained as to its results. Again and again is the hope expressed by officials who ruled in India in the first half of the 19th. century that British schools would be a bulwark of strength to their Empire. They clearly recognized that the pen must retain what the sword had won. The question addressed by the statue of Lawrence in Lahore to every passer-by, "Will you be governed by the sword or pen ?" is misleading. It conceals the truth that we are governed by both sword and pen.

I now quote a few extracts from various sources to illustrate the feelings with which the Government regarded their educational policy in its early days. Mr. Charles Grant in his book on the education of the Indian people, published in 1792-97, remarked : "In success would lie our safety, not our danger."

We shall take the most rational means to remove inherent great disorders, to attach the Hindu people to ourselves, to ensure the safety of our possessions, to enhance continually their value to us.

(Chapter IV).

Sir C. Trevelyan, a relative of Lord Macaulay's who served the East India Company in various capacities and rose to be Governor of Madras Presidency and Member of the Supreme Council in India, wrote a book "On the Education of the People of India" in 1838. He discussed the question of education from all standpoints and came to the conclusion that a million sterling annually expended on the education of the Indians would "render them at once to our rule and worthy of our alliance." He remarked with profound wisdom :

In following this course we should be trying no new experiment. The Romans at once civilized the nations of Europe and attached them to their rule by Romanizing them, or, in other words, by educating them in the Roman literature and arts and teaching them to emulate their conquerors instead of opposing them. Acquisitions made by superiority in war were consolidated by superiority in the arts of peace and the remembrance of the original violence was lost in that of the benefits which resulted from it. The provincials of Italy, Spain, Africa and Gaul, having no ambition except to imitate the Romans, and share their privileges with them, remained to the last faithful subjects of the Empire, and the union was at last dissolved, not by internal revolt, but by the shock of external violence, which involved conquerors and conquered in one common overthrow. The Indians will, I hope, soon stand in the same position towards us in which we once stood towards the Romans. Tacitus informs us that it was the policy of Julius Agricola to instruct the sons of leading men among the Britons in the literature and science of Rome, and to give them a taste for the refinements of Roman civilization. We all know how well this plan answered. From being obstinate enemies, the Britons soon became attached and confiding friends; and they made more strenuous efforts to retain the Romans than their ancestors had done to resist their invasion.

We may also take a lesson from the Mohammadans whose conquests have been so extensive and permanent. . . .The Emperor Akbar followed up this policy in India. Arabicised Persian was adopted as the language of his dynasty, and the direction thereby given to the national sympathies and ideas greatly contributed to produce that feeling of veneration for the family which has long survived the loss of its power.

The Rev. Alexander Duff, the father of Christian Education in India, published a pamphlet in 1837 offering an "Exposition of the late Governor-General of India's last Act." (viz., the Education Act of 1835). The learned missionary remarked :

When the Romans conquered a province, they forthwith set themselves to the task of Romanizing it; that is they strove to create a taste for their own more refined language and literature, and thereby aimed at turning the song and the romance and the history, the thought and the feeling and the fancy, of the subjugated people into Romon channels, which fed and augmented roman interests. And has Rome not succeeded ?

The Great Akbar established the Persian language as the language of business and polite literature throughout his extensive dominions, and the popular tongue naturally became deeply impregnated with it. The literature and the language of the country thus became identified with the genius of his dynasty, and this has tended more than anything else to produce a kind of intuitive veneration for the family, which has long survived even the destruction of their power, and this feeling will continue to exist until we substitute the English language for the Persian, which will dissolve the spell, and direct the ideas and sympathies of the natives towards their present rulers. (p. 27).

Sir Alexander J. Arbuthnot, K.C.S.I., who was for some time a Member of the Supreme Council of India, remarked in the course of the Convocation address he delivered to the students of the Calcutta University in 1880 :

My conviction is that the more thorough and the more complete the education is which we impart to the people of India, the better fitted they will be to appreciate the blessings of British rule and the more they will deprecate any material change in the existing order of things.

Sir Richard Temple, Bart., in his well-known book "India in 1880," says :

Of late certain symptoms of disloyalty manifested by some limited sections of certain educated classes, have caused reflections to be made against the effects of education upon native loyalty. But that disloyalty was traceable to social and traditional circumstances quite apart from educational causes, and was checked, not fostered or encouraged, by education. There doubtless will be found disloyal individuals among the educated classes as there are among all classes in a country subjected to foreign rule. Nevertheless, a well-founded assurance may be entertained that those natives who have learned to think through the medium of the language and are imbued with the literature and the philosophy of England, will bear towards the English nation that heartfelt allegiance which men may feel without at all relinquishing their own nationality.

The same distinguished Anglo-Indian writes in another part of the book :

The harder questions relate to the effects of education on the conduct of these men, on their trustworthiness and integrity, their loyalty to the British sovereign, their gratitude to their foreign instructors, their attachment to Western civilization, and their sentiments in regard to the existing order of things. The answers to such questions, if thoughtfully rendered, will be found as satisfactory as could be fairly anticipated.

It should be noticed that two officials declared after fifty years' experience of the effects of British education, that it was a source of strength to the British connection. The rulers of 1835 hoped and prophesized : the officials of 1880 saw the realization of that hope and the fulfilment of that prophecy.

So much for the general aims of British educational policy. It may be asserted that the British considered it their duty to improve and civilize India by strengthening their rule and Anglicising us in our social life, intellectual pursuits and political attitude. I do not wish to enter upon a discussion of this point at present. I set forth what history teaches. Let every one arrive at his own conclusions.

Let us go a little into details. How could the educational system strengthen the foundations of English rule in India ? How was it that the civilian found an ally in the schoolmaster ? Mr. P. M. Mehta thus describes the relation between a British soldier in the Indian army and a teacher in an Anglo-Vernacular Government school :

In India, gentlemen, the soldier is abroad and must be: but the humble schoolmaster is no less indispensable. He alone can add stability and permanence to the work of the soldier.

(Speech at Bombay Graduates' Association. April 4, 1893)

Let us examine the process by which a B.A.,B.T. contributes his share of work towards the consolidation of British authority in India. The whole scheme was as clear as daylight to the founders of the educational system.

First: The educational system brings Indians into close contact with Englishmen and thus encourages mutual regard and esteem. It weakens the feelings of aversion and contempt with which all conquered nations at first regard their foreign rulers, who are different from them in religion, manners and language. It promotes social intercourse between the rulers and the ruled, and softens racial animosities. It cuts at the root of the instinctive repugnance born of patriotism, with which all races regard their conquerors in the period immediately following the conquest when the sores are not healed and bitter memories separate the two communities like a river of blood. Thus the educational system supplies a point of contrast between the rulers and the ruled. The pupil can not divest himself of all respect for his teacher. The violence of racial hatred and prejudice on the part of the ruled is really tempered and allayed by the relations that subsist between the teacher and the taught.

The gift of knowledge tends to blunt the edge of resentment felt at the loss of national dignity and self-respect. The process undertaken by the ruling power resembled the task that lay before Jahangir after he had got rid of Shah Jahan how to attach Nur Jahan to himself? We know that Nur Jahan refused even to see her husband's enemy for some time. But patience and policy overcame all obstacles. And the recalcitrant widow became the charming empress in due time. Thus Sir C. Trevelyan wrote in 1838 :

The Arabian or Muhammadan system is based on the exercise of power and the indulgence of passion. The earth is the inheritance of the faithful. The Hindu system, although less fierce and aggressive than the Muhammadan, is still more exclusive: all who are not Hindus are impure outcasts, fit only for the most degraded employments, and of course utterly disqualified for the duties of Government, which are reserved for the military, under the guidance of the priestly caste. Such is the political tendency of the Arabic and Sanskrit systems of learning. Happily for us, these principles exist in their full force only in books written in different languages and in the minds of a few learned men; and they are very faintly reflected in the feelings and opinions of the body of the people. But what will be thought of that plan of national education which would revive them and make them popular; would be perpetually reminding the Muhammadans that we are infidel usurpers of some of the fairest realms of the faithful and the Hindus that we are unclean beasts, with whom it is a sin and shame to have any friendly intercourse. Our bitterest enemies could not desire more than that we should propapate systems of learning which excite the strongest feelings of human nature against ourselves.

Thus Sir C. Trevelyan pointed out in 1838 that the Arabic and Sanskrit educational systems then in vogue in India encouraged national exclusiveness and racial hatred. He went on to say :

The spirit of English literature, on the other hand, cannot but be favourable to the English connection. Familiarly acquainted with us by means of our literature, the Indian youth almost cease to regard us as foreigners. . . . . .From violent opponents or sullen conformists, they are converted into zealous and intelligent co-operators with us.

Referring to "the young men brought up at our seminaries," Sir C. Trevelyan says :

Instead of regarding us with dislike, they court our society, and look upon us as their natural protectors and benefactors :

the summit of their ambition is to resemble us.

Thus British schools and colleges were actually expected to work a miracle, to convert the sons of those who had fought the English in battle into apt and docile pupils who should regard their Christian rulers as their guided and Gurus. What a change!

Lord Ripon in 1882 said :

That object is, in the main, to bring together and unite the European and the native in the common pursuit and the common love of knowledge.

Lord Mayo hinted at the effect of the educational system in overcoming the feelings of repugnance which naturally prevented the Indians from mixing with Europeans :

I am not without hope that perhaps in the establishment of the school, the college and the University, we may be weaving a golden band which may bind in closer union the subjects of our Queen, be they dark or fair, whether they reside in the East or the West."

(Address at Calcutta in 1869).

The British rulers realized that, in establishing a common platform on which European and Indian could meet and shake hands, they were strengthening their position in the country. They were drawing the coy Hindu maiden out of the safe zenana of national social exclusiveness in which she had concealed herself away from the sight of unruly admirers.

Thus Sir William W. Hunter, in his book on "The Indian Mussalmans" (published in 1871), enucnciated a general principle in these words: "The chronic peril which environs British Power in India is the gap between the Rulers and the Ruled."

Let us ponder over the profound wisdom of this proposition and understand how the educational system helps British influence by bridging the gulf between white and brown, and breaking down the barriers, which Hindu exclusiveness had erected between aggressive conquerors of various races and creeds and the weak, divided and spiritless Hindu community.

The consolidation of British rule in India could also be helped by alienating the people, or at least the intelligent and Wealthy classes among them, from their national habits and manners, language and literature and then "improving" and "civilizing" them by teaching them to follow the example of their conquerors. This process of Anglicisation could be initiated through the agency of schools and colleges which should instil the new ideas and tastes into the minds of the young men of the nation. This purpose is distinctly avowed by Macaulay in his famous Minute of 1835 about which Mr. C.H. Cameron, President of the Calcutta Council of Education, declared that it "may be considered as the immediate cause of the resolution of Government which settled this great question," This Minute on Education—a document which no thinking patriot can refer to in terms of praise or appreciation—contains sentiments like the following :

"The question now before us is simply whether, when it is in our power to teach this language (viz. English), we shall teach languages (viz. Sanskrit and Arabic) in which, by universal confession, there are no books on any subjects which deserve to be compared to our own".

"That literature" (i.e. Sanskrit) inculcates the most serious errors on the most important subjects."

"Books which are of less value than the paper on which they are printed while it was blank" (i.e. Sanskrit books).

These extracts illustrate the spirit in which one of the chief founders of the British educational system set about his work. He declared, plainly and unequivocally :

We must at present do our best to form a class who may be interpreters between us and the millions we govern; a class of persons Indian in blood and colour but English in taste, in opinion, in morals and in intellect.

He confidently looked forward to the day when Britain would have established "the imperishable empire of our arts and our morals, our literature and our laws," in India. This "imperial" sentiment closes the well-known passage which is often quoted with delight by many politicians and in which he admits the possibility of the establishment of "European institutions" in India after some time. The Right Hon'ble Charles Grant, in his treatise published in 1792-7, remarked:

"Certainly in a political view the great question which this country has to determine respecting India is 'What are the best means of perpetuating our empire there?'

"At present we are every way different from the people whom we hold in subjection : different in country, in language, in manners, in customs, in sentiments and in religion : their interests also. . . .they must conceive to be different from ours. What, then, can be a healing principle with regard to all these points, but a principle of assimilation, a common bond" (the itelics are original) "which shall give to both parties the reality and the conviction of mutual benefit from the connection. Without a uniting principle, a conjoining tie of this nature, we can suppose the country to be, in fact, retained only by mere power, but in the same degree that an identity of sentiments and principles would be established, we should see a sight new in the region of Hindustan, a people actively attached, cordially affected to their Government and thus augmenting its strength."

Mr. Grant then quotes Dr. Robertson to show how Alexander "early perceived, that to render his authority secure and permanent", he must Hellenise his Asiatic subjects, who should "become one people" with Europeans "by obeying the same laws and by adopting the same manners, institutions and discipline." Mr. Grant adds : "It is the leading idea only of this policy, that is meant to be applied here : and that leading idea is plainly the principle assimilation."

Mr. Grant does not wish that the "distinctions between the two races" (in India) "should be lost." He only desires "to attach our subjects by affection, by interest, by winning them to our religion, and our sentiments. That would have the effect of rendering our authority permanent and secure."

Evidently Mr. Grant proposed that we should not become completely English in all respects but should cease to be Hindus, thus losing the privileges of both civilizations. He wanted to turn out hybrid outcastes.

Sir Charles Trevelyan wrote in 1938 :

"Educated in the same way, interested in the same objects, engaged in the same pursuits with ourselves, they become more English than Hindus, just as the Roman provincials became more Romans than Gauls or Italians. What is it that makes us what we are, except living and conversing with English people and imbibing English thoughts and habits of mind. They do so too; they daily converse with the best and wisest Englishmen through the medium of their works, and form perhaps a higher idea of our nation than if their intercourse with it were of a more personal kind."

The founders of the British educational system in India ardently desired the triumph of the English language all over the world. Sir Charles Trevelyan thus summed up the views of the advocates of English education in 1838 on this point :

"With a partial exception in Canada, English is the language of the continent of America, North of Mexico. . . . In the West India Islands, we have given our language to a population collected from various parts of Africa. . . . . Their literature will be the literature of England. More recently the English language has taken root in the continent of africa itself and a nation is being formed by means of it in the extensive territory belonging to the Cape. But the scene of its greatest triumphs will be in Asia. To the South a new continent is being peopled with the English race; to the North an ancient people who have always taken the lead in the progress of religion and science in the East have adopted the English language as their language of education. . . . . The English language, not many generations hence, will be spoken by millions in all the four quarters of the globe, and our learning, our morals, our principles of constitutional liberty, and our religion, embodied in the established literature and diffused through the genius of the vernacular languages, will spread far and wide among the nations."

Professor H. H. Wilson, the famous scholar, wrote a letter to a journal in 1836, in which he said :

"I have noticed for some time past repeated effusions in the Calcutta newspapers, advocating a departure from principles hitherto considered sound and just, and recommending the exclusive encouragement of English as the first stage of a very feasible project for the annihilation of all the languages of India, vernacular or classical, and the universal use of our native tongue throughout the East. As long as the reveries were confined to the columns of a newspaper they were inoffensive or even amusing; they assumed more importance when, in order to prepare for the extermination of the languages, the suppression of the alphabets was seriously undertaken and Oriental works were printed in characters which the natives could not read."

The hope was also expressed that the social life of the Indians would be transformed. Thus the Right Hon'ble Mr. C. Grant said :

"Let them acquire a relish for the ingenious exertions of the human mind in Europe, for the beauties and refinements endlessly diversified, of European art and science."

Mr. Grant also spoke of the time when the "English manners, tastes and wants must also have become common."

Mr. Charles Hay Cameron was President of the Council of Education in Calcutta in 1845. The Council, under his guidance, prepared a plan for a University at Calcutta about which, among other things it remarked :

"It would encourage the cultivation of the arts and sciences, and call into existence a class of native architects, engineers, surveyors and educated land-holders whose influence would rapidly and certainly diffuse a taste for the more refined and intellectual pleasures and pursuits of the West."

Finally, as regards religion, which is the greatest social force in existence, which provides the sanction for almost every rule of conduct and supports the permanent institutions of society in all countries, Elphinstone, the first English Governor of Bombay, expressed his ideas in these memorable words :

"To the mixture of religion, even in the slightest degree, with our plans of education, I must strongly object. I am convinced that the conversion of the natives must infallibly result from the diffusion of knowledge among them. Evidently they are not aware of the connexion, or all attacks on their ignorance would be as vigorously resisted as if they were on their religion. The only effect of introducing Christianity into our schools would be to sound the alarm and to warn the Brahmans of the approaching danger."

It is about Elphinstone that the pathetic story is related how he told Gibbs that the education of Indians "was our high road back to Europe."

Mr. Charles Grant's allusions to religion have been quoted above. He also remarked, in another part of his treatise :

"It might be too sanguine to form into a wish an idea most pleasing and desirable in itself, that our religion and our knowledge might be diffused over other dark portions of the globe where Nature has been more kind than human institutions. This is the noblest species of conquest."

The Report of the Committee of Public Institution, dated December 1831, noted with satisfaction that :

"The encouragement of the Vidyalaya or Hindu College of Calcutta has always been one of the chief objects of the Committee's attention. The consequence has surpassed expectation. A command of the English language and a familiarity with its literature and science have been acquired to an extent rarely equalled by any schools in Europe. The moral effect has been equally remarkable; an impatience of the restrictions of Hinduism and a disregard of its ceremonies are openly avowed by many young men of respectable birth and talents and entertained by many more who outwardly conform to the practices of their countrymen."

Thus we find that a Commitee appointed by Government and consisting of responsible officials delights in the notion that the Hindu youths manifest an aversion to their ancestral faith and its sacraments. Elphinstone, in a Minute, dated 13th December, 1823, has pointed out a possible danger to British rule from the religions of India :

"In the meantime the dangers to which we are exposed from the sensitive character of the religion of the natives and the slippery foundation of our Government. Owing to the total separation between us and our subjects, require the adoption of some measures to counteract them; and the only one is to remove their prejudices and to communicate our own principles and opinions by the diffusion of a national education."

Sir Charles Trevelyan, in his deposition before a Select Committee of the House of Lords, on the 28th. June, 1853 said :

"The Bible is not admitted as a class book into Government seminaries. This rule has been objected to, as implying hostility to the progress of Christianity; but no opinion was ever more mistaken. When we formed English libraries in connection with the different Government institutions, on the reorganization of the system of instruction, after the resolution of 1835, the Bible was placed in all the libraries, and I understand that it is now desired that Mant's and other commentaries on the Bible should also be placed there, thereto I see no objection . . . . .If we look at actual results, it will be found that of the well-educated converts to Christianity, nearly as many have come from the Hindu College and other Government institutions as from Missionary seminaries. Our text-books on moral philosophy are wholly Christian in their spirit and tendency. In Abercrombie's "Intellectual Powers," which is carefully studied without curtailment, there is a distinct chapter on the evidences of Christianity."

Sir Frederick Halliday, an eminent Bengal Civilian, who was Secretary to the Government of India and afterwards became Lieutenant-Governor of Bengal, gave evidence before a Select Committee of the House of Commons in 1853. In reply to the question whether the Bible should be introduced as a class-book in the Government schools, he said :

"If anybody says. . . .that the Bible is 'systematically prescribed or 'authoritatively prescribed,' I cannot understand the meaning of it; persons who write in that way must mean something which I am unable to fathom or they are not acquainted with the facts. It is not true that the Bible is prescribed in the Government schools; it is put into the Government school libraries universally, and the students are allowed, to the top of their bent to read it from beginning to end. . . . It has been truly said by Sir Charles Trevelyan, in the Committee of the House of Lords, that we are not conscious ourselves to the full extent of the amount of Christian teaching involved in a thoroughly classical English education, independently of all direct efforts at conversion. It renders necessary a knowledge of the Bible and I may say a knowledge of the great doctrines of Christianity. . . . I believe there is more knowledge of the Bible in the Hindu College of Calcutta than there is in any Public School in England."

Sir W. W. Hunter, Director-General of Statistics to the Government of India, remarked in 1872 :

"No young man, whether Hindu or Muhammadan, passes through our Anglo-Indian Schools without learning to disbelieve the faith of his fathers. The luxuriant religions of Asia shrivel into dry sticks when brought into contact with the icy realities of Western Science."

He also proposed that, as a remedy for Muhammadan disaffection and fanaticism, a system of Anglo-Arabic schools should be established by the Government. He thus described its advantages:

"We should thus at length have the Muhammadan youth educated upon our own plan. Without interfering in any way with their religion, and in the very process of enabling them to learn their religious duties, we should render that religion perhaps less sincere, but certainly less fanatical. The rising generation would tread the steps which have conducted the Hindus, not long ago, the most bigoted nation on earth, into their present state of easy tolerance. Such a tolerance implies a less earnest belief than their fathers had.... I do not permit myself here to touch upon the means by which, through a stae of indifference, the Hindus and Musalmans alike may yet reach a higher level of belief. But I firmly believe that that day will come and that our system of education, which has hitherto produced only negative virtues, is the first stage towards it. ("The Indian Musalmans" : p. 214).

In the above extracts, the italics are mine, except where the contrary is indicated.

It is clear that the educational system was expected and intended to produce a revolution in all our institutions, our language, our customs and manners, and our religion, and thus to produce a large and growing "class of persons, Indian in blood and colour, but English in taste, in opinions, in morals and in intellect." (Macaulay's Famous Minutes, 1835).

The process of "Assimilation" to a foreign race, which is popularity known as "denationalization", continues to work. In the meantime, the Government has to look to its safety and stability. A foreign Government must try all means in its power to prolong its existence. It is exposed to so many dangers from all sides that it has been often compared to a settlement on the edge of a volcano. Hence the Government must influence the thoughts of the people according to its conception of what is good and proper. Ideas rule in the world.

"A thinking man," said Carlyle, "is the worst enemy of the Devil." The mind of the nation cannot be left to itself. Laws and Regulations are passed in order to ensure physical order and peace. But the Mind submits to no Arms Act. It is above coercion. No Government can forcibly compel a man to think in a particular manner. The body can be restrained or controlled by power; but who shall forge a fetter for the National Mind and Spirit?

And yet it is clear that unless a Government can control and guide the Thoughts and Opinions of its subjects, it connot be said to have provided for its security. It may order the newest guns and build the most massive forts but its work is incomplete till it has brought under subjection that which is more powerful than all the armies of the world put together—the Mind and Will of a nation which has not lost its vitality.

The educational system provided the Government with a potent means of guiding and moulding the opinions and activities of our young men. It really served to crush our national "aspirations" and divert our energies into various channels approved by authorities. The necessity of destroying the ideas of national dignity and freedom was patent to the officials who ruled India immediately after the fall of the old dynasties. Thus Sir Charles Trevelyan remarked in his book on Education published in 1838 :

"These views were not worked out by reflection, but were forced on me by actual observation and experience. I passed some years in parts of India, where owing to the comparative novelty of our rule and to the absence of any attempt to alter the current of native feeling, the national habits of thinking remained unchanged. There, high and low, rich and poor, had only one idea of improving their political condition. The upper classes lived upon the prospect of regaining their former pre-eminence; and the lower, upon having the avenues to wealth and distinction reopened to them by the re-establishment of a native government. Even sensible and comparatively well-affected natives had no notion that there was any remedy for the existing depressed state of their nation except the sudden and absolute expulsion of the English. After that I resided for some years in Bengal, and there I found quite another set of ideas prevalent among the educated natives. Instead of cutting the throats of the English, they were aspiring to sit with them on the grand jury or on the bench of a Magistrate. Instead of speculating on Punjab and Nepalese politics they were discussing the advantages of printing, and free discussion in oratorical English speeches at debating societies which they had established among themselves."

So we find that the British Schools and colleges were founded to wean our "uneducated" ancestors of the early 19th century from the pernicious habit of "speculating on Panjab or Nepalese politics" and to suggest to them ways and methods of progress more peaceful and "civilized" than the "sudden and absolute expulsion of the English". They were to dispel that perverse ignorance, on account of which the people had "only one idea of improving their political condition." Why could they not form societies for the protection of children and associations for the dissemination of correct knowledge about lice and worms as a preliminary to national regeneration ? Poor folk, they were not "educated", and so possessed only one great national "aspiration", the longing for freedom.

Sir Charles Trevelyan pointed out that it was necessary to guide the patriotic and public spirited people among Indians along right lines lest they should stray into undesirable paths. Even our patriotism was to be made to subserve the purposes of Anglo-Indian officials, who were, of course, our "well-wishers." Let our youngmen reflect on the following :

"There is a principle in human nature which impels all mankind to aim at improving their condition : every individual has his plan of happiness : every community has its ideas of securing the national honour and prosperity. This powerful and universal principle, in some shape or other, is in a state of constant activity; and if it be not enlisted on our side, it must be arrayed against us. As long as the natives are left to brood over their former independence, their sole specific for improving, their condition is the immediate and total expulsion of the English. A native patriot of the old school has no notion of anything beyond this : his attention has never been called to any other mode of restoring the dignity and prosperity of his country. It is only by the infusion of European ideas that a new direction can be given to the national views. The young men brought up at our seminaries, turn with contempt from the barbarous despotisms under which their ancestors groaned. . . . Instead of regarding us with dislike, they court our society. . . . So far from having the idea of driving the English into the sea uppermost in their minds they have no notion of any improvement but such as rivets their connection with the English and makes them dependent on English protection and instruction." (Sir C. Trevelyan in 1838).

Sir Charles was of the opinion that if the English "set the natives on a process of European improvement," the results would be most gratifying to the rulers.

"They will then cease to desire and aim at independence on the old Indian footing. A sudden change will then be impossible; and a long continuance of our present connection with India will ever be assured to us. A Mahratta or a Muhammadan despotism might be re-established in a month; but a century would scarcely suffice to prepare the people for self-government on the European model. The natives will not rise against us. . . . The national activity will be fully and harmlessly employed in acquiring and diffusing European knowledge and in naturalising European institutions. The educated classes, knowing that the elevation of their country on these principles can only be worked out under protection will naturally cling to us. They even now do so. There is no class of our subjects to whom we are so thoroughly necessary as those whose opinions have been cast in the English mould."

Thus we see that while the old uneducated men of seventy years ago did not know any plan of "restoring the dignity and prosperity" of the nation which did not involve the expulsion of the English from India, the efforts of the Government to give "a new direction" to the "national views" resulted in the production of a class of men who were poles asunder from their fathers, as they could not hit upon any scheme of national improvement which did not make them "dependent on English protection." What a revolution in the public opinion of the country was brought about by the simple process of gathering our young men in classes and suggesting to them new lines of thought and action which lead them away from the political ambitions and aspirations of their fathers! Thus did Government mould the Indian mind immediately after the establishment of the British dominion. At a time when, according to high official authority, "a Mahratta or Muhammadan despotism might be re-established in a month", it was essential for the consolidation of the empire that the national intellect should be brought under proper control, lest we should "brood over our former independence"—a most objectionable and unpatriotic pastime from all stand-points, and particularly so in the eyes of the officials! Sir Charles Trevelyan's words should open the eyes of those who fancy that a denationalising and demoralising educational system has produced, for the first time in the history of India, a "national awakening" which makes men think of freedom. It has had exactly the opposite effect, as is clear from the unimpeachable historical testimony quoted above. Alas the puppets should be unconscious of the presence of the wire-puller!

Charles Hay Cameron, Member of the Council of India and President of the Council of Education for Bengal, published "An Address to Parliament on the Duties of Great Britain to India in 1853." He urged the establishment of Universities in the country and remarked he should "endeavour to frame to himself a distinct notion of the social and political condition into which it should be our object to bring our Indian empire by the combind forces of legislation and public instruction." Thus the schools and colleges were to be the instruments for the dissemination of particular ideas of "progress" and "reform among our people". He recommended "an imperial scheme of education" for India.

Sir Charles Trevelyan had clear ideas as to what was required for the army, which he called "the pillar of our Indian Empire." He was of the opinion that the educational system was a means of promoting loyalty to the British among the military classes.

"The instruction given to the labouring classes can never be more than merely elementary. They have not leisure for more. But, such as it is, they will be indebted for it to us; and as it will form part of a system established and superintended by ourselves, we shall take care that it is of a kind calculated to inspire feelings of attachment to the British connection. After this, the young men who enlist in the army will become imbued with the military spirit and moulded by the habits of military obedience. I leave to others to judge whether this training is calculated to make better and more attached, or worse and more disaffected, soldiers than the state of entire neglect, as regards their moral and intellectual improvement, in which the whole class are at present left."

The safety of every foreign government requires that the rulers should try to associate the intelligent and the influential section of the conquered nation with themselves in the work of "government". No foreign government which desires to provide for its stability, can afford to ignore the wealthy and the cultured classes among the subject people, for it is men of good birth and education who can guide their countrymen and lead them to glory or to ruin as they choose. The leaders of the people must be propitiated; they should be persuaded to identify themselves with the new regime. Unless they definitely throw in their lot with the conquerors, they will be the rallying points for all malcontents who wish to restore the old state of affairs. Their association with the ruling race serves to curb the spirit of the masses and deprives the opposition of its most valuable allies, the natural leaders of the nation.

Hence the foreign government always tries to give the aristocracy of the conquered country some share in the administration of the new State in order to make them and others forget the old times which they had seen. This policy of conciliation is eminently suited to serve the interests of the rulers, for conciliation and consolidation go hand in hand. Large empires are generally based on the passive acquiescence of the common people combined with the active and interested support of the influential classes among the conquered races. How to secure the latter requisite of stength and security is the great problem that confronts every Empire builder. So it was with Rome. So it was with Akbar. So it was with the conquerors of India in the early days of the 19th century. History repeats itself.

The association of the subject people in the administration also gives the ruling race the opportunity of acquiring social superiority over the conquered races. Victory in battle confers only military and political supremacy on the rulers. But the acceptance of offices in the administration by important members of the ruled races places within the reach of the new-comers the boon which they ardently long for, viz., a definite place in the social system of the country. They do not desire to occupy a position of social inferiority; they would not sit below the salt. The only method by which they can supplement their merely military occupation with the acquisition and assertion of social superiority in every day life is the association of rich and learned "natives" with the foreign Government, i.e. the bestowal of posts under the Executive Head of the alien Administration on proud and patriotic nobles and scholars.

The Court of Directors of the East India Company, in a despatch to the Government of Madras dated 29th September 1830, wrote :

"You are, moreover, acquainted with our anxious desire to have at our disposal a body of natives, qualified, by their habits and acquirements, to take a larger share and occupy higher situations in the Civil Administration of their country than hitherto been the practice under our Indian Governments."

The Court of Directors, in a Despatch to the Governor-General in Council of Bengal declared :

"In the meantime we wish you to be fully assured, not only of our anxiety that the judicial offices to which natives are at present eligible should be properly filled, but of our earnest wish and hope to see them qualified for situations of higher importance and trust. There is no point of view in which we look with greater interest at the exertions you are now making for the instruction of the natives than as being calculated to raise up a class of persons, qualified, from their intelligence and morality, for high employments in the Civil Administration of India. As the means of bringing about this most desirable object, we rely chiefly on their becoming, through a familiarity with European literature and Science, imbued with the ideas and feelings of civilized Europe, on the general cultivation of their understandings and specifically on their instruction in the principles of morals and general jurisprudence. We wish you to consider this as our deliberate view of the scope and end to which all our endeavours with respect to the education of natives should refer."

The despatch of the Court of Directors to the Government of Bombay, dated 29th September, 1830, contained the following :

"It is our anxious desire to afford to the higher classes of the natives of India the means of instruction in European science and of access to the literature of civilized Europe. The character which may be given to the classes possessed of leisure and natural influence ultimately determines that of the whole people. We are sensible, moreover, that it is our duty to afford the best equivalent in our power to these classes, for the advantages of which the introduction of our Government has deprived them; and for this and other reasons of which you are well aware, we are extremely desirous that their education should be such as to qualify them for higher situations in the Civil Government of India, than any to which natives have hither-to been eligible."

Sir John Malcolm, Governor of Bombay, wrote a Minute in 1828 on the question of Education in India. He said :

"One of the chief objects, I expect, of diffusing education among the natives of India, is our increased power of associating them in every part of our administration. This I deem essential on grounds of economy, of improvement, and of security.

I cannot look for education of expense in the different branches of our Government from any diminution of the salaries now enjoyed by European public servants, but I look to it from many of the duties they now have to perform being executed by natives on diminished salaries."

A Despatch of the Court of Directors of 1827 urged "the importance of raising up educated natives of high moral character for the discharge of public duties", and added with remarkable candour :—"To this, the last and highest object of education, we expect that a large share of your attention will be applied."

So it is discovered that the "highest object of education" is the creation of a class of "native" servants for a Foreign Government ! We recommend this grand ideal to those educationists who hanker after University degrees.

Section 72 of the Famous Despatch of 1854, which some politicians, who are fond of dealing in "Charters" for subject races, call "The Educational Charter" of India, explicitly establishes a close connexion between the educational system and the "public" services :

"We have always been of opinion that the spread of education in India will produce a greater efficiency in all branches of administration, by enabling you to obtain the services of intelligent and trustworthy persons in every department of Government, and on the other hand, we believe that the numerous vacancies of different kinds which have constantly to be filled up may afford a great stimulus to education."

Section 73 of the same Despatch indicates the desire of Government to obtain efficient servants in larger numbers :

"We understand that it is often not so much the want of Government employment, as the want of properly qualified persons to be employed to Government, which is felt at the present time in many parts of India."

The Government not only desired to give offices to the aristocracy, lest Satan might 'find mischief for the idle hands to do,' but it also intended to secure a supply of inferior officials at a cheap rate. A tropical country governed by Europeans cannot afford to employ Europeans who demand large salaries before they can undertake a life of royal exile. Hence it is expedient, as Sir John Malcolm recommended, to utilize the services of Indian clerks and daftries, who work for the Government on a mere pittance. All the dirty drudgery of the State offices is to be borne by them. The magnificent fabric of the Empire is to rest on the labours of "sweated" middle-class literate Indians. This class should be made as cheap for Government as possible.

"From English schools being established at no place but Bombay, the pay of writers and accountants is immoderately high, and when these move from the presidency they require still higher wages; and when well-qualified, they can from their limited numbers, command almost any pay they demand. This introduces a tone of extravagance of damand from this class of person in all our departments. Of some remedies of this evil, I shall speak hereafter; but the real mode to decrease price is to multiply the article. English school be established or encouraged at Surat and Poona."

(Minute by Sir J. Malcolm, Governor of Bombay, 1829)

The employment of the upper classes in the administration is recommended with a view to conciliate and compensate them, while the association of the middle classes in the work of "government" serves a different purpose. It enables Government to use their powers of mind and body for its own benfit with is little expense to itself as possible. A system of sweating at the bottom surmounted by a system of conciliation at the top, constitutes the essence of the policy of "associating the natives in the administration". The policy of conciliation is also described by some acute and malevolent critics as a policy of Bribery and Demoralization. But what's in a name so long as we understand the truth?

(c) The creation of a "dependent class is one of the main objects of the eductional system. A foreign Government must find some basis of support within the conquered community, otherwise it will be short-lived. It tenure of power will be precarious indeed, if it cannot succeed in inducing some classes among the subject people to identify their interests with the ruling caste. A large number of people, who depend for their rank and subsistence on the favour of any Government, are in duty bound to support it at all times. Their conduct will always be controlled by self-interest. A partition wall of Bread and Butter will divide them from their countrymen. There can be no such class of persons in a country at the time when it is conquered. The new rulers are complete strangers to the people. In course of time they manage to raise a servile caste from among the people, a caste which knows no law higher than the fiat of its employers, no duty more sacred than obedience to the powers that be. It attaches itself to the foreign Government as a dog follows its master for meat. It consents to justify and "interpret" all actions of the Government for the benefit of its subjects. It serves as the medium through which Government can carry out schemes with which it does not wish to associate itself openly. It is the tool of the conqueror, an obliging, supple, unscrupulous, astute, avaricious and hypocritical caste of "Government Servants", devoid of principle, of self-respect, of patriotism. It may be recognized as a caste composed of cruel, cowardly, cunning, cringing, covetous and characterless persons. It is distinguished from other classes as being pre-eminently the characterless caste. This is its great characteristic. The production of such a caste within the social system of the Hindus was, in the words of the Court of Directors, the "last and highest object" of the educational system established by the East India Company. C. H. Cameron, President of the Council of Education in Bengal, said in 1853 :

"The class that we are creating, as we approach towards this great object,—the class imbued with European letters—will be for many generations wholly dependent upon us, much more so than any of the separate and antagonistic classes which we found already extinguished; and they will exceed all those other classes in their enlightened perception of their true position, still more than in the degree of dependence which characterizes it."

The advocates of the English Educational system in the early years of the nineteenth centuary also looked forward to an increase in the Indian demand for European goods as an consequence of the spread of education in India. Thus the commercial instincts of the ruling race enabled it to realise that the system might "improve" the "natives", but it would certainly enrich the Europeans. Mr. Charles Grant, in his treatise on Indian Education written in 1792-97, said : "In every propressive step of this work, we shall also serve the original design with which we visited India, that design still so important to this country the extension of our commerce. Let them acquire relish for the ingenious exertions of the human mind in Europe for the beauties and refinements, endlessly diversified, of European art and science, and we shall hence, obtain four-and-twenty millions of distant subjects. How greatly will our country be thus aided in rising still superior to all her difficulties, and how stable as well as unrivalled may we hope our commerce will be . . .Wherever we may venture to say, our principle and language are introduced, our commerce will follow."

We have described the objects of British "educational" policy in order that our countrymen may obtain an insight into the principles which the British Government has followed in rearing the magnificent system of Universities, Colleges and schools of various descriptions, before which some of us stand speechless with admiration and gratitude.

History teaches us that all conquering races attempt a social and intellectual conquest of subject races after they have secured political dominion over them. The political conquest only destroys the organized physical strength of a weak nation. But the process of social and intellecutal subjugation corrupts and poisons its national life at its very source. It kills the soul of the nation, it robs it of its individuality as a race. It thus renders its political regeneration impossible.

The British rulers of India have only followed the lesson taught by History. They have had considerable experience in the art of conquering other peoples. They have also been conquered by several nations in the early period of their history. They have not exhibited any superhuman sagacity and cunning in thus sapping the foundations of our nationality. All "imperial" races know the trick : it is a device with which all aggressive and vigorous nations, not excepting the Hindus in the days of their glory, have been familiar, Let us see how the "educational" systems of different conquering nations have affected their subjects.

Rome : The Romans have been the greatest and the wisest "imperial" race on earth. The name of Rome is a synonym for empire. Rome consolidated her empire and attached her subjects to herself by offering them Roman art and culture. The national individuality of the Gaul and the Briton was thus destroyed. No country under Roman dominion ever produced a national literature of its own. The provincial scholars tried to excel in Latin, the language of the ruling race. The grandchildren of the British chiefs who had resisted the Roman invasion of Britain took pride in wearing the toga and speaking the Latin tongue.

The Aryans : The Hindus were great warriors and conquerors in the days of their youth. They colonized and civilized the whole of India and established their rule over countries which are described as the abode of Vanaras and Rakshasas in the Ramayan. The spread of Hindu dominion over the continent was the work of our great ancestors. They too perpetuated their rule over the subject races by Hinduizing them, by conquering them socially and intellectually. They taught their subjects the Sanskrit language, converted them to the Hindu religion and completely transformed their socil life. Nothing of the old "barbarism" remained and the "national" feeling of the tribe also disappeared. Thus did our forefathers consolidated their empire. They were wise men in their generation.

Islam : The fact that Muhammadan conquerors insisted on a complete revolution in the life of the nations who fell before them is known to all. Persia and Afghanistan lost their old civilizations and were Muhammadanized. India was partially brought under Islamic influence, as we had more resisting power than the Iranians. Akbar laid firm the foundations of the Mogul Empire by teaching us Persian, which gave birth to Urdu. If Urdu had not been invented, how could the descendants of those who fought Babar read the poems composed by Zafar, a representative of his dynasty, with delight and appreciation? The study of Persian literature by some classes of Hindus was a source of strength to the Muhammadan State. Those Hindus who thus abjured their ancestral speech must have lost something of the fine patriotic feeling that animated the heart of a Brahman, to whom everything associated with Islam was an abomination.

Spain : Spain has had a large colonial Empire. She left the impress of her civilization on her dependencies. The inhabitants of the Phillippines still cherish the Spanish language and the Roman Catholic faith which they had received from their conquerors. Even to-day Portugal is looked upon as the mother country by colonies who are now politically independent but whose reverence for Common,the Portugal, links them to Portugal with an indissoluble chain.

England & Ireland : The disastrous effects of the British educational system in countries which have been conquered by the pushing Briton are best illustrated by the havoc it has wrought in Ireland. In India the evil has not gone so deep, as the Hindus possess a strong national individuality and the educational system has found its admirers only among the upper classes as yet. The British Government established schools in Ireland in 1830. They were designed for the purpose of denationalizing the Irish race and thus impairing their power of resisting the foreigner. All the text books except one were prepared by Scotchmen and Englishmen. Irish history and poetry were proscribed. Mr. O'Brien, in the Home Ruler's Manual, informs us that Scott's poem "Breathes there a man with soul so dead" was removed from the text-books to make room for these beautiful lines illustrative of British truthfulness and British poetical genius :

"I bless the glory and the grace
That on my birth have smiled
And made me in these Christian days,
A happy English child."

The Irish children were to dishonour their parents and the memory of their ancestors by reciting these lines in the schools. Mr. Sidney Brooks, in his book "New Ireland," is of opinion that the British educational system all but destroyed the Gaelic language, which is now confied to the suburbs but which was universally spoken in Ireland a hundred years ago. The Irish language was ignored, if not actually penalized in the foreign system. The impartial English author bears testimony to ruinous effects of the British educational system in destroying Irish national games and pastimes, music and culture. The national individuality of the race almost perished. The children did not know the history of their nation. They could not acquire a thorough command of the English tongue and they forgot their own language. The thread of historic continuity was suddenly snapped in these hybrid outcastes who were divorced from their own civilization and could not assimilate another. And with the decay of their language and institutions, "the true fibre of Irish manhood began to rot away." Moral and intellectual stagnation set in. A mob of slaves without a memory of their past was the product of their educational system which found the Irish people with a national civilization and left them without one. Thus the Irish acquired a little "knowledge" at the cost of their national life. They sacrificed the end for the means.

Now, after a century of painful experience, the Irish have been awakened to a sense of their miserable position. They have formed the Gaelic League to revive the old language and music, the old games and customs.

America & Cuba : To come to the history of our own times, America is trying her best to Americanize her new subjects in Asia and Australia. Persons who crave free and compulsory education as a boon from the Government should take note of the fact that the Americans granted this "concession" to the Cubans and the Hawailans of their own free will immediately after the conquest. The American Government even supplies the text-books free of charge in Cuba! Thus these islanders are being civilized away. A letter from the Director of Education in Porto Rice to the supervisors of English education contained the following injunction :

"Supervising the teaching of English in Porto Rico, which you now undertake, is one of the most important duties of the hour."

It is stated in the Report of the Commissioner of Education, U.S.A., that the want of a knowledge of English was the greatest difficulty in the way of those who wished to become American in thought, culture and loyalty.

Germany and Poland : At present a conflict is raging between the German authorities and their Polish subjects on this vital question of education.

1. *National Institutions.* National Institutions are the sign and symbol of national individuality. All men have the organs of sense; the intellect, affections, feelings, passions, love and hate, jealousy and sympathy, avarice and philanthropy are common to all civilized people. All men eat and drink, wear clothes and talk to each other, take part in the religious worship of some sort or other, and pay homage to some historical past. The essence of national life consists in the particular religion which we follow, the particular history

which we cherish, the particular language that we love and speak, the particular social life which we appreciate. Language, social life, religion, literature, history—these form the living forces in a community which mould national character and aspirations. It is for their protection and preserva tion that we create the State, the army, the navy and the police. It is for the defence of these beloved institutions, the heirlooms which we have inherited from our ancestors, that we desire to attain Swaraj. It is for these sacred treasures that every nation sacrifices ease and wealth and life from generation to generation. They form the nerves and fibres of the organism called the State. They constitute the foundations of the National Polity. The nation decays when we cease to love them with a passionate all-absorbing love.

National institutions are thus the essential marks of national life. There can be no Nation without national institutions. It is mere moonshine to talk of 'nationality' when there are no living institutions corresponding to the idea of nationality. Nationality is kept alive and strengthened by real institutions which are a part and parcel of our daily life which we have been taught to love and revere from childhood. It is not fed on speeches, aspirations, arguments, imagination, cosmopolitanism and such like in substantial stuff. An exposition of Bluntschli's theory of nationality will not infuse into him a keen feeling of nationality, If his daily life teaches him to despise, or neglect national institutions, he can never be patriotic. Experience is a more efficient teacher than words and logic.

Now let us see how the British educational system de-Hinduizes us and causes the decay of our national institutions, thereby hindering the growth of the feeling of Hindu Unity and national life.

(i) *Language* : Language is a most important national institution. It is often the distinguishing feature of nationality. A Dutch proverb says, No language, no nationality. Language is the bond of society. It marks off our countrymen from the stranger. Bhasha is also the mother, as the Ganga is the Mother, for without Bhasha we cannot live even for a day.

Language not only unites the men of the present generation and enables them to deliberate together on national affairs, but it also enables us to hold communion with the dead. It is the key to national history. The words and deeds of our forefathers are enshrined in out language,—in Sanskrit, Hindi and Panjabi—like pearl in a shell. National language thus preserves historical continuity, which is the life of the nation. A common historical background is one of the indispensable conditions of national growth. Common political ideals and aspirations are impossible without a common past.

Language is also the guardian of the national literature, which voices the national spirit. A nation's literature is one of its most precious possessions. Carlyle has written that if he were asked to give up the Indian Empire or Shakespear, he would gladly forego the former, but not the great national poet of England. The Empire, he says, must go some day, but Shakespear represents the eternal, imperishable wealth of England.

It is language then that preserves and interprets National History and Literature. It stands sentinal at the gate of the National Temple and no one who does not answer its call "Who goes there" can enter the sacred precincts.

The effect of the British educational system on the National Language is disastrous.

The Hindu nation has two languages which it should teach to every member of the race. One is an imperial language : the other is the provincial tongue.

Corresponding to the double consciousness of tribal and of national unity, we have two languages for every cultivated Hindu who wishes to discharge his duty towards his country. There is the Sanskrit, the language of Empire and Religion, the imperial and sacred language of the Hindus; and then comes the Vernacular, the tribal tongue of different provinces,

Hindi, Bengali, Marathi, etc. When a Hindu addresses the whole nation he uses Sanskrit; when he confines himself to his own particular province, he employs his vernacular. Sanskrit embodies the common imperial past of the nation.

How does the British educational system affect our languages, Sanskrit and Hindi or Marathi or Gujrati ? One fact will enable us to realize the situation better than a whole page of exposition.

I, an educated Hindu, am writing an article in English in this paper and communicate my tought not to Englishmen or Americans but to my own friends and countrymen, living in the same province and the same country and speaking the same language as myself.

The series of articles is the most conclusive proof of the disastrous effects of this educational system on our languages.

If I had followed nature, if our whole life had not been rendered ridiculous, artificial and miserable by this educational system, I should have written in Sanskrit to appeal to my countrymen in Bengal, Bombay or Madras (an aspiration which has not altogether been abandoned) and in Hindi to address the people of my province.

I take this occasion to apologize to the Ancestor and to my countrymen of the present generation for thus dishonouring and weakening a national institution. My only excuse is that the pernicious habit of reading newspapers and magazines published in English which prevails among our upper classes compels me to address them through the medium of the language of a foreign country situated 7,000 miles away from Lahore. The upper classes are the brain of the nation. If we wish to rescue a man from a bog we have to enter it ourselves and give him a helping hand. It is for this reason that I stoop to compromise my national dignity by indulging in this artificial and ludicrous practice.

(ii) *History* : National History is the sine qua non of national unity and growth. A national that has no past must lack cohesion and patriotism. Common hero-worship is the bond of society.

The British rulers of India teach our boys what is really a caricature of Hindu history. The text-books written by the Lethbridges and Hunters of the Anglo-Indian community give us no idea of our ancient greatness. They impress on the minds of our boys notion that we have been an incapable race since the dawn of history and that our only function has been to lose battles one after another in the course of centuries. There is no mention of all that should be the pride of every Hindu.

Woe to the nation that allows its children to read history as it is written by its foreign conquerors ! No people with a particle of self-respect would tolerate it even for a moment. We may be unable to emulate our ancestors : but let us at least refrain from reviling them.

A man who sends his son to an Anglo-Indian school commits the sin of pitri-ninda, the vilification of national heroes, the dishonouring of national history.

(iii) *Literature* : Language and literature go together. Sanskrit literature must lose ground before English if the present system endures. Our boys have to study Scott and Milton, while they are utterly ignorant of Sanskrit literature, which is equally inspiring and artistic. English is already taking the place of Sanskrit as the medium of communication among Hindus belonging to different provinces. English is a compulsory subject for all classes at school and college. The Hindu nation must choose between Sanskrit and English. Under the present system Sanskrit literature and learning will gradually perish and with its decay will fall the whole edifice of Hindu civilization. For our society draws its morality and religion, its social spirit and its laws, from the Shastras. The decline of Sanskrit learning will reduce us to the condition of a disorganized mob without national institutions.

Ayurveda is being undermined by Government Medical Colleges. A Hindu youngman can become a "graduate" in

Philosophy without reading anything of Hindu metaphysics the highest product of Hindu genius ! Religion is proscribed in Government schools. The study of the Upanishads and the Smrities is no part of the University curriculum.

The British education system will destroy Sanskrit literature and learning which is the pride and glory of our race and the well-spring of our moral and social ideals.

This unnatural system will also kill out our vernaculars. Already we see the sorrowful spectacle of parents writing letters to their children in English, of people reading newspapers in English, of students giving English name to their clubs and associations, of national assemblies possessing English names ! There are thousands of Hindus in Oudh who have received "education" at Anglo-Indian schools, and can not therefore read the Ramayan with facility. The language of the people is system-atically ignored in the University curriculum. It is the case of Ireland over again. Instead of teaching the boys through medium of their own language, the Anglo-Indians compel them to answer examination papers in history and geography in English ! I wonder if English boys at Eton learn history from text-books written in Chinese. With literature will go our culture and art. Indeed, the decay of Hindu intellectual life is patent to all who have eyes to see. Sir George Birdwood makes the following candid confession : "We are destroying their faith and their literature and their arts, and the continuity of the spontaneous development of their civilization and their great historical personality; in a word, we are destroying the very soul of the nation."

(iv) *Social Life* : Social life is a national institution. It grows and changes like all other institutions. But it is all times a determining factor in national life. It is the product of the instinct which leads all nations to adapt themselves to their surroundings. It creates the environments in the midst of which it is possible for national intellect and morals to grow and develop. A natural healthy social life, suited to the time and place, is a national asset of the greatest value.

Social life is also a mark and symbol of national unity. It should not be tampered with in an irreverent spirit.

The British educational system throws our social life out of gear. It upsets all rules and conventions and weakens our sense of social duty. It leads to indescribable confusion in dress, modes of speech and rules of etiquette. The climax is reached in such instances as that of the man who said, on entering a temple, "Good evening, Vishnu!". Many young Hindu take to shaving their moustache even when they are not in mourning for the loss of their parents. Others might insist on being buried after death. A few have married European wives without converting them to Hinduism. The national social life is thus thrown off its hinges. The Muhammadans gave at the first shock from which it has not been able to recover. The present educational system tends to disorganize and destroy it altogether.

Thus the "Educational" system established by Anglo-Indians saps the vitality of national institutions, which are the source of national feeling and aspiration.

(v) *Character* : What idea does not the British educational system represent? And what ideal does it inculcate? If it does not stand for any great idea and does not touch a great ideal, it must have a ruinous effect on Hindu character. Ideas and ideals quicken the moral life of a people. The only idea which it may be said to represent is the acquisition of a knowledge of the language : the only ideal that it seems to place before us is that of becoming a graduate.

Idealism : the soul of an individual's moral life, has no place in this system, for it deliberately excludes religion from its curriculum. And it does not teach national history either. Religion and patriotism are the two great forces which have made men great in different countries and ages. An educational system which does not value either of them must produce men without an ideal and without backbone!

Hence the students of our colleges have no faith in anything—religion or politics or art or science. They believe only in things of the world. Those among them who have risen above materialism or moral inertia have come under the influence of powerful forces originating outside the Anglo-Indian educational system. The majority of our graduates have lost the fine old faith of their fathers in Hindu social institutions and have not found any other moral basis of life. The Truth that was does not appeal to them : and they have not caught a glimpse of the Truth that shall be. And where there is no vision the people perisheth.

Patriotism : must decay under a system which discourages the study of our national past. British 'educational' policy alienates the cultured classes from the common people, diminishes their reverence and love for great heroes like Rama, Krishna and Guru Govind, and curbs their political aspirations. Mr. Gokhale tells us that Mr. Ranade wrote an essay depreciating the British system of Government in comparison with Mahratta rule, "Sir Alexander Grant, who was then Principal of Elphinstone College, and who had great admiration for Mr. Ranade's talents, sent for him and after pointing out to him the error of his views, said to him : 'Youngman, you should not thus run down a Government which is educating you and doing so much for your people.' And to mark his serious displeasure he suspended Mr. Ranade's scholarship for six months."

The Government has turned its colleges into comfortable prisons for our youngmen, who are prevented from reading nationalist newspapers and attending meetings at which sound political ideas are promulgated. Woe to those who lose their birthright of learning about the condition of their country and honouring the greatmen of the nation for a mess of pottage in the shape of a license for practice at the Bar or a Government diploma of graduation! They sacrifice the end for the means: they lose the substance and run after the shadow. They demoralise themselves and teach others to do violence to their conscience. Thus the British educational system promotes servility, cowardice and social decay. Sir W. Lee Warner, in his little book "The Citizen of India", teaches our boys the following precious truth :

"There is no 'drain' of wealth from India to England. The former rulers of India never cared for their people.

India is growing in prosperity under British rule."

Men who send their sons to School where such books are taught injure the nation and betray their trust as guardians of their children.

Courage is not a quality which can grow in the unhealthy moral atmosphere of our colleges. Students who have to show respect to officials for whom they have really no love in their hearts, cannot possess any moral courage. A life of Fraud and Falsehood can never build up character. The strain which the artificial method of teaching through the medium of English puts on our energies undermines our physical stamina and exhausts out vitality even before we enter on the struggle of life.

As to the minor virtues which have adorned Hindu character from time immemorial, simplicity, temperance, courtesy, family affection, and respect for elders, the British 'educational' system is notoriously fatal to their development.

Patriotism and spirituality—the two great character—making forces—are absent from this "educational" system. The smaller virtues which are also inherited by Hindus, decay through the influence of ill-digested European ideas and the example of third-rate European professors.

The Hindu character is ruined. The springs of the national moral life are poisoned. If a man gain the world, but lose his own soul, what shall it profit him? So said a teacher of old. And if a nation should acquire the learning of the whole world but lose its life, its institutions and its character, how will it survive ? We cannot give our life in exchange for a smattering of English literature and Science. We cannot consent to part with our nationhood for such paltry advantages.

The British Educational System is the present of two great evils—Denationalization and demoralization. It weakens Hindu social and religious institutions and it undermines patriotism and moral courage. No device could be more effectual for accelerating our decline as a nation.

There are several other consequences of the establishment of Government schools and colleges which deserve notice:

(a) *The Social Degradation of the Hindu race* : The Briton, having acquired the power and glory which belonged to the Kshatriya, tries to step into the place held by the Brahman in order that he may complete the social conquest of India by England. Political and Military predominance must be supported by social supremacy, otherwise it can not endure. A nation, which has only lost its national State, is not crushed, it is under a merely temporary eclipse. But if it should gradually lose the sense of self-respect and national individuality by mixing with foreigners on terms of inequality, it can not rise again. Political subjection is not so grave an evil as social serfdom to Europeans.

Schools and colleges convert our Brahmans, Kshatriyas and Vaisyas into docile and respectful pupils of Christians and Anglo-Indian officials. The conquerors get an opportunity of posing as teachers and benefactors of the "subject" race. Our boys learn to occupy a position of social inferiority to Europeans in everyday life, for the teacher must always sit above the pupil. They begin to look up to members of the conquering race as their moral and spiritual guides. Thus does Brahmanhood too pass from the Hindu Brahman to the Englishman. Another victory in the conflict of civilization is won by the Briton. The Brahman who should teach our children, is displaced by the pushing foreigner. The social conquest proceeds apace, killing out national pride and self-respect and the feeling of national identity along our upper and middle classes.

All "low-abiding" subjects of the British Empire are required to pay taxes and obey the laws established by the Government. No man is compelled to do more for the bureaucracy. How mean and unpatriotic must those people be, who voluntarily accept the discipleship of the bureaucracy and become not only subjects but also pupils and social inferiors to Anglo-Indiadom.

(b) *The prestige of the burecracy* : The Government of India should control and guide all activities in Hindu society, if it wishes to enhance its prestige and take the place of an earthly Providence in the mind of the people. The educational system adds to the prestige of the officials who manage it. They stand forth before the public as instructors and receive spontaneous homage from unthinking men who do not understand their policy. A Government school in a village impresses on the imagination of the people great truth that the Sirkar is an all-powerful, all-absorbing, omni present and omnicient agency controlled by men of wonderful power and wisdom. The Sirkar is a very Ishwara on earth: it is here, there and every where: it does so many things and does them well. Verily, saith the rustic philosopher, the Sirkar is the only reality in the world: all else is maya. It has no hands, but it works; it has no eyes but it sees. The Sirkar is the source of all Life.

(c) *The Loss of Self-Government* : A subject people should at least try to keep the direction of their social affairs in their own hands as far as possible. All interference on the part of foreigners, even if it is well-meant, should be nipped in the bud. The political and military activities of the nation must pass under the control of foreigners as a necessary consequence of subjugation. But we need not give them all when they ask only an inch. Those who send their sons to Anglo-Indian schools are following the stupid policy of surrendering to Government more than it demands of us as a conquering power : Education, Religion and Social customs should form the sacred circle within which all unhallowed foreign control is inadmissible. The British Government does not compel us to resort to its schools. Why should we give up the duty of managing our own affairs in these spheres of national life and activity which are still under our own control. The British Educational system will destroy Kashi, Nuddea, and other centres of Hindu learning. It robs us of our capacity for self-government in educational matters. The old-world Pundit who opens an "indigenous" school on his own account practises self-government on a small scale. But enlightened public men who patronize Government Colleges, help the extension of bureaucratic influence in our social life. Cursed be those who destroy the small remnants of self-government which a jealous and grasping bureaucracy still allows to a subject people. We have lost much: we have fallen. Why should we lose more and fall lower? Why should we give up the privilege of self-government in Educational affairs?

It should be clearly understood that all extension of Government control and supervision involves a corresponding decay in the vitality of the people. Everything that is done by the bureaucracy must take something out of the hands of the people. Government control and initiative must be fatal to the growth of the capacity for self-government among the nation. This is self-evident. Light must recede as the shadows advance. Even a beneficial institution established by Government impairs our power of establishing and managing it through our own energy and enterprise. The loss of self-government, even if accompanied with a temporary advantage. is to be dreaded like a calamity, for it saps the moral qualities which are necessary for complete self-government and which it should be our duty to foster. When it brings in its train other evils, it is of course an unmitigated course. A public library established by Government only hinders the growth of popular civic life while it confers a temporary benefit on us. Even a pathshala or a temple which is established by Government for the promotion of Sanskrit learning is injurious to our national interests for it undermines the habits of self-help and self-reliance, which alone can save the Hindu race and its religion. But Government schools and colleges rob us of all that we hold dear—self-respect, character, patriotism, national literature and history, and finally self-Government in educational affairs.

(d) *The Extention of British Influence in Indian States* : The Universities have been efficient instruments for driving the thin end of the wedge of British influence into the affairs of Indian States. It is no where provided in any treaty that a ruling Indian Prince should connect the schools and colleges of his State with the British Universities. Yet we are so foolish that we cut at the root of our own national life by sending up our boys in the States for University Examinations. The Government is not to blame in this respect. It does not compel any Raja or Nawab to place his educational department in partial subordination to the British Educational Service. Our incapable and indolent Ministers have of their own free will compromised the dignity of our States and impaired their vitality by allowing and even asking the British Universities to extend their operations in their territory. Is it impossible for states which collect their own revenues and administer their internal affairs in all departments, to establish their own schools and colleges under the sole authority and guidance of the Head of the State ? As I observe the humilitating spectacle of an Indian State requesting British Universities to exercise control and authority in their Colleges, I am reminded of Raja Sir T. Madhav Rao's pregnant words :

"The longer I live, observe and think, the more deeply do I feel that there is no community on the face of the earth which suffers . . . . more from self-invited, self-accepted or self-aggravated, and therefore avoidable evils than the Hindu community."

(I am quoting from memory)

(e) *The Industrial Backwardness of the Nation* : The British educational system serves to convert the sons of our bankers, traders and land-owners into dependents of the bureaucracy whlle the field of industrial and commercial enterprise is left open for the European settlers in India. The University curriculum prepares our youngmen for no useful profession. It encourages literary culture but proscribes commercial training and technical studies. Mr. Chesney has recognized this defect of the British educational system in his book on "The Indian Polity", The inevitable effect of that system is the creation of an ever-increasing class of useless persons, who know no art or trade and who are compelled to serve the administration as officials or lawyers in order to earn a'living. The foundations of our economic life are thus undermined. It is sad, indescribably sad, to see sons of shopkeepers and bankers trying to "rise" in the social scale by taking to the profession of a lawyer. They suffer from a strange perversion of judgment. The imagine that a lawyer or an official is entitled to greater social esteem than an honest shopkeeper or landowner. The educational system tends to incapacitate our youths for a commercial or industrial career. It smooths the path of the European exploiter before him. It will turn the children of our Vaishyas into hangers-on the bureaucracy, lawyers and officials while European capitalists are getting our trade and industry more and more into their hands. The process of dethroning the Vaishya from his pedestal of financial power and installing the European planter or merchant or banker in his place is in progress. And the Universities help materially in the process. They facilitate and accelerate the economic enslavement of our race.

Having shown the numerous evils that flow from the unnatural and artificial educational system which the British have established in India, I now proceed to expose certain fallacies which are current among many "educated" people with regard to its effects on our character and progress. It is wonderful that we Indians accept wrong ideas and ideals without a word of protest. We are lacking in the critical faculty. With regard to the educational problem, we have been living in a sort of fool's paradise, hugging the chains that have bound us. It is time that we should clear our minds of cant.

It is a favourite notion with many patriots that this system with its insistence on English literature as a compulsory subject of tuition, provides us with an instrument of communication between the different Indian people which are divided by differences of language. This system is supposed to have conferred a common language, the sina qua non of the Indian unity, on our people. With its progress, therefore, the cause of Indian Nationalism is bound up in a definite manner. The English language is regarded as the future lingua franca of India. Thus it is imagined that the conquest has conferred this inestimable boon on us.

This India is most pernicious. It implies an absurdity. It contradicts the teachings of history and sociology. It is derived from a superficial study of post-Mutiny Indian politics. It is a product of the minds of ill-informed students of sociology devoid of insight into Reality.

If English is to be the language of unified India, then it appears that a united India means a denationalized India. The great semi-independent States like Nepal, Udaipur and Hyderabad cannot boast of a denationalised and demoralised class of "Graduates" such as are turned out by British Universities, in India. They still cherish the national language and need not forget it to make English the language of public business. The states are under no necessity of sacrificing Indian culture and civilization. They are and ought to be the bulwarks of the national civilization against the attacks of alien ideals. Hence those politicians who set up English as the language of United India confine their attention to "British" India that portion of our country which has been completely subjugated by foreigners. They do not think of those Indians who still enjoy some of the elementary rights of humanity, of which we who live in British India have been deprived. It would be a curious plan of union which should omit to consider the people of the States which enjoy a large measure of self-government.

Then, again, the principle which insists on the adoption of the conqueror's language for our national purposes is radically unsound. It is destructive of national solidarity. It may, under certain circumstances, cut at the root of our national existence altogether. It is an accident that the great majority of Indians have fallen under the dominion of one European power. The fact conceals from us the dangerous nature of the programme which would base unity on a foreign language. There are some Indians who are subjects of the French Republic. Others own allegiance to Portugal. What shall we do with these fellowmen of ours? Shall we shun them altogether simply because they are not "British" subjects? Are they comprehenced in our plan of union? Those Politicians who adopt English as the lingua franca of India evidently believe that Indians who have not been conquered by Britain have no part or lot with us. They see only the red colour on the map of India. If India were to be partitioned among different European powers a contingency which did not appear impossible in the eighteenth century, the Anglicised politicians would call several Congresses transacting business in various European languages. For, according to them, the language of the conquering race provides the principle of Unity in this chaotic mass of languages and dialects. The plan would be fatal to the very existence of the Hindu nation.

This consideration brings me to the great truth which I wish to emphasize. The principle of Unity exists WITHIN a community and cannot be imported from WITHOUT. All uniformity produced by the adoption of external devices is deceptive. It will not lead to unity, as will lack the quickening soul which keeps an institution alive. If all Indians were to speak Esperanto which is a much easier language to learn than English that would not stimulate national feeling or preserve national institutions.

Let us not be deceived by the glamour of the present or base our national movement on the errors of a purblind generation. Decades are as moments in the history of a nation. The illusion of Anglicisation, from which we have been suffering for the last thirty years, must be destroyed. The Brahma of National Self-Realization is hidden from us where this Maya prevails. Sanskrit is the only national tongue for all India—the language of our noble religion and the tongue associated with India's highest hopes and happiness. It is the medium of inter-communication among the various States, and it is the language of science and scholarship. It speaks to us of our common past and can furnish the only solid foundation for a genuine national movement. Why should I seek proficiency in English if I do not want to be a lawyer or a servant of the British Government ? A tolerable knowledge of that language, or even French or German, would give me access to stores of modern civilization. But I must learn Sanskrit will in order to join the ranks of the educated classes in India. No Hindu who is ignorant of Sanskrit can have any pretensions to culture.

But some people say that Sanskrit is a dead language, and that it cannot be commonly used for purpose of national business. This idea is altogether erroneous. It is easier for a hindu to learn Sanskrit than English. Sanskrit is not dead—it is we who are dead. Of course, we cannot deliver lectures before the Britith public in Sanskrit. We cannot write articles to advise and inform the Bureaucracy in Sanskrit. But those who wish to teach the people and build up a nation, must part company with those who traffic in unreal political charlatanism. Those who desire to make a great and united Nation must take their stand on Sanskrit as the eternal refuge and glory of the Indian people.

We have got into the habit of writing and speaking in English on public affairs. There is really no reason why a graduate who knows both Sanskrit and English should not use the former where he now employs the latter. Sanskrit will come to him more naturally than English. But it is a fatality pursuing all conquered races that they dig their own graves. The Hindus of Northern India voluntarily gave up Sanskrit and took to Persian under the Mogul regime, and a similar suicidal policy is being pursued at present on a vaster scale.

There is another error which has found acceptance in all circles and which is, if possible, even more grotesque and disastrous. The idea is abroad that the British educational system is the parent of Progress. It is supposed to have conferred on us poor benighted Asiatics the great notions of liberty, political enfranchisement, social advancement, and what not. It is said to have verified our decaying civilization rescued us from the slough of despondency into which we had fallen. It is the mother of "New India". Shall we kill the hen that lays the golden eggs ?

The advocates of the British educational system assume too much. They have to prove that a system which teaches no religious ideals and discourages patriotism can confer any benefits on a people. They must show that the English-educated classes have brought about any political awakening I think that our political aspirations have been curbed and crushed by this system. The ideal of co-operation with the bureaucracy—which means playing second fiddle only—as the summum bonum of Indian humanity, could be evolved only out of the dwarfed imagination of half-educated men who could not think clearly and boldly. The tree is judged by its fruits. The vast majority of those who have been educated at schools and colleges are continually engaged in undermining the foundations of their nationality. They serve as assistants to the bureaucracy, as teachers in Government schools, as lawyers and barristers in British courts of law, and thus enhance the prestige of the bureaucratic rulers of the country. They are helping in the destruction of the national genius for original and independent pursuits. That is what the "English-educated" class is doing—it is dragging the nation to a lower level in the scale of humanity by accepting the ideals, the discipleship, and the patronage of the bureaucracy. It has been truly said that if there were not a poor and ignorant peasantry on one side and unpatriotic "educated" class on the other, things in India would be different from what they are at present.

A few men here and there have escaped the soul-corroding, denationalizing influence of this educational system chiefly through the agency of various religious movements which, of course, cannot owe their origin to British schools and colleges. These few men have not learnt the lessons of sacrifice and spirituality, moral courage and patriotism, at the feet of Anglo-

Indian officials who teach in the Colleges. For of thorns men do not gather figs. The innate vitality of Indian civilisation is not yet exhausted, otherwise there would be no hope for us. That civilisation has given us the few great men we have produced in the 19th century—Ranjit Singh, Dayanand, Ram Krishna, Salar Jang, Vivekanand and a few others. How can the soulless instruction given in the Anglo-Indian schools produce great men? The effects of Anglo-Indian education were seen in the first generation of Bengalis who were turned out from Government Colleges—a set of fashionable, denationalized, unpatriotic, selfish creatures, the very scum of Indian humanity thrown up to the surface by official patronage. Scores were converted to Christianity. Since then the old Hindu civilivation has asserted itself against the baneful effects of this system, and the evil has been to some extent counteracted.

But we must devise a thorough cure for this malady. It has been asserted that the ideas of "liberty" and "nationality" have been conferred on us by this Anglo-Indian system. These ideas are said to be peculiarly Western products, and the study of Mill and Thomas Paine is supposed to have fired our hearts with a passion for freedom. Mr. S. Nair, who is now a Government servant, cried : "You cannot urge a man into slavery in the English language." Mr. Gokhale is of opinion that the "new spirit" has been produced by the education imparted at Government schools and colleges.

It would be strange, passing strange, if such ideas as those of liberty and nationality could grow in the servile and denationalizing atmosphere of Government colleges. And how has Afghanistan got such a firm hold on these great ideas ? How have the Gurkhas acquired their intense love of liberty ? Our "educated" men have learned a few quotations from Burke and Mill; they have read sonnets in praise of Liberty. But of the real thing, patriotism, many of them know as little as the man in the moon. Why, a man who possessed European ideas of patriotism and national self-respect would never send his sons to schools that lead to denationalization.

And some of us serve the bureaucracy and then prate of "national" unity ! Parrots repeat Vedic Mantras and the holy name of liberty is dessecrated in the mouths of men who talk glibly of patriotism while helping the bureaucratic regime as lawyers and officials ! As for our "Congressmen", they seem to have lost the primary instincts of self-respecting nations. They think they have learned the lesson of patriotism" at British schools and colleges. Queer "patriotism" indeed which makes its votaries regard it glory to occupy a position of permanent inferiority playing the second fiddle again-to Englishmen in the "constitution of the Government !

The Fallacy of The "Awakening" : The Indian National Congress is often supposed to be the outcome of the British educational system. And it is taken for granted that the Congress is a monument of wisdom and patriotism. It follows therefore that the political progress of India depends on the British educational system.

Is the Congress a sign of political progress or of decay ? Does it represent an advance in political ideas and methods, or does it imply a retrogression in the political life of the nation ? This point must be settled before we can pronounce on the merits and demerits of the British educational system, as it is believed in some circles that the Anglo-Indian colleges have led to a great political awakening, which is symbolized by the Congress. This erroneous idea has not been got rid of even by some Nationalists.

If the Congress were the quintessence of the Indian Nation's wisdom and patriotism, I should be very doubtful as to the future of that nation. The Congress marks a retrograde step in the political life of India, and the British educational system is responsible for the decline in India's political morality and sagacity which made the Congress possible. For such an assembly could not exist in a country where natural feelings of self-respect and pride had not been undermined by some cause or other. Why could there be no Congress in the year 1820 or 1860 ? Let us reflect on this question. The year 1884, in which the Congress was founded marks the period when Indian intelligence and national feeling fell prostrate before the systematic assaults of Anglo-Indians, and the people ceased to hope for any serious improvement in their political status and condition.

Let us analyse the idea for which the Congress stands or stood. The ideal of association with the bureaucracy which has been proclaimed by the Congress in the resolutions, and the agitation in favour of simultaneous examinations and the admission of Indians to high offices in the service of the British Government, clearly represent a sad decay of national self-respect and of the ethical standard of the nation.

Let us not be misled by appearances. We some times deceive ourselves that we are more civilized than our grand-fathers because we hold so many meetings, deliver speeches in the right Royal London style, and possess newspapers and journals. But noise is not life. We know the proverb which says that empty vessels make much noise. Maharashtra boasts of many newspapers, dailies and weeklies, while Nepal and Afghanistan do not enjoy the luxury of newspaper reading. But which has more true and vigorous national life Maha-rashtra or, Afghanistan? Some of us have learned all the beauties of the theory of nationality, but are the Gurkhas politically in a worse condition than the Bengalis simply because they cannot discourse on the blessings of liberty? We must penetrate through the shows of things to the reality. We have to find out if our views and methods are superior to those which the "uneducated" people of the early nineteeth century appreciated and advocated for the political progress of the country.

As to the methods of political work, the majority of the English-educated classes shrink from self-help and national self-assertion. They believe in oratory and pursuation. They have preached for twenty years and more that the only method of political advancement is the use of the tongue and the pen to the exclusion of other instruments. They have degenerated into mere poltroons and windbags, and want to impose their wrong ideas on the sturdy peasants who know that politics is not a war of words between bureaucrats and their courtly disciples. They know the essential principles of politics and are not deluded into erroneous opinions like the English-educated wiseacres who deliver eloquent speeches before the English tailors and cobblers and grocers.

The idea of "agitation" for political purposes was altogether unknown to our ancestors who lived before the era of schools and colleges, for they never suspected that a disarmed nation could work out its salvation by the use of its tongue and lungs. They did not imagine that vast gatherings of cowardly serfs, even if held everyday would induce Government to relinquish any of its powers and privileges. They never made any mistakes on fundamental questions like the nature of British rule, the character and aims of the British people, the need of maintaining social and political isolation from the rulers, the futility of mere words in political matters and the future destiny of India. On all these points, their ideas were sound and natural.

But strange and absurd opinions have been manufactured in Government colleges under the guidance of clever Anglo-Indians and are now held up to our admiration as tokens of a great "political awakening," as symbols of a "new spirit" of which Messrs Surendranath Bannerjee, Ranade, Mehta, W.C. Bonnerji and others are the apostles. These men were the "englightened ones," the leaders who dispelled the "darkness" in which brave old-fashioned peasants and Rajas wandered blindly about, and who inaugurated the era of "light and progress". Let us examine what the "awakening" was like. What were the antecedents of the "leaders" who had emerged from the colleges with the new gospel of political puerility and emasculation, which was to be preached from the platform of that small body with a big name "The Indian National Congress".

Mr. Surrendra Nath Banerji, the orator of the "awakening," established a college for which he could not find the name of any Indian hero, and so had to fix on Ripon. He praises Alexander Duff, the Christian missionary, in terms of warm appreciation. Then again he pleaded for simultaneous examinations, which should enable more Indians to ruin their country by joining an aristocratic service which holds itself aloof from the masses. Mr. Ranade was thrice invited to accept the honour and dignity of the Dewan of large Hindu States, but his denationalized proclivities led him to cling to his post under the British Government, This was the "new spirit", which taught Hindu scholars to prefer subordinate places under the British to honour and power under a Hindu Raja in a free State. Mr. Mehta is so great a friend of India that he called the British educational system "a great boon," while at the same time he was convinced that this system would clear the way for Christianity." (Mehta's Speeches--Ed. by Chintamani)). He was the man who uttered that blasphemous sentence which makes every Hindu burn with shame :

"Lord Ripon, Lord Buddha styled on earth".

This champion of the "awakening" compared a Christian Viceroy to, a Hindu avatar, one of the greatest men, if not the greatest man indeed, that the world has yet produced. He also declared that "his faith was large even in Anglo-Indians". And, last but not least, we have Mr. Gokhale one of those patriots who could not choose a better name for the college which was supported by their noble self-sacrifice than that of an English Governor of Bombay.

So much for the apostles of this "new" dispensation which has been the product of British schools and colleges and which postulates permanent subordination and inferiority to Englishmen as its ideal.

We need not study history to find out that the "education" imparted in Government schools and colleges has blinded us to the Primary truths of political science which were clear as day light to those noblemen and peasants who had not come under Anglo-Indian influence. We may look around us to-day and discover that the "uneducated" unsophisticated people still possess sound ideas on important questions like the essential nature of British Rule and the methods of political work. The artisans of the towns and the peasants in the villages look upon the British as a strange people who will not mix with them and with whom they should not mix. In their hearts they are convinced of the superiority of their fine old civilisation. They have shown their political capacity and insight on many occasions, The repeal of plague regulations, the prohibition of the sale of beef in a manner which offended the religious susceptabilities of the Hindus, belief for the indebtedness of the Deccan ryots—these and other necessary reforms have not been obtained through the efforts of the orators and politicians of the Congress school but have been due to the spontaneous united action of the masses of the people. Had the common people sat at the feet of the Congress "leader", they would never have succeeded in remedying the evils from which they suffered.

Thus recent history also proves that the illiterate peasants and townsmen have more commonsense and insight than the English-educated graduates who have preached the gospel of the so-called "awakening". The people know how to help themselves, whatever the misguided platform speakers may say.

The much-talked-of political "awakening" which has been traced to the education given in Government Schools is a myth and a delusion, This blessed educational system has given birth to the class of political buffoons mimics who expose us to the ridicule of the world by preaching the association with the bureaucracy in the administration is the panacca of all our social and political ills, and that a fallen nation does not need self-help, self-respect, and the power to stand on its own legs for its political regeneration.

3

Role in Freedom Movement

It is not easy to discuss within the limits of a short essay the salient characteristics of German society as it presented itself to an Oriental traveller during the war. I have spent about three and a half years in Germany and Turkey during the war; and I now jot down my personal impressions for the benefit of the people of India and Egypt. I speak from direct personal experience. I shall not quote from books and newspapers. I relate what I have seen with my own eyes and heard with my own ears. The history of Germany during the last forty-eight years has been a record of folly ending in failure; and this war has been a German crime ending in a German catastrophe. My personal views and reflections may be useful to the educated classes of India. Egypt, and other Oriental countries.

Oriental readers may ask how it was possible that such an active and well-instructed nation should have made the mistakes and committed the sins which have brought a just Nemesis on it. I shall try to answer this question, extenuating nothing and setting down naught in malice. I am a cosmopolitan in spirit, and can judge and criticise with an unbiassed mind.

The Germans are intellectually not behind the other European nations but they are morally, socially, and politically in a lower stage of development. They are a well-instructed, semi-barbarous nation, and resemble a Berber or a Kurd, who should somehow acquire a knowledge of advanced science and literature without thereby divesting himself of his primitive habits and ideas. In Germany one finds a strange and startling mixture of rampant mediaeval barbarism and up-to-date modern civilisation. Intellectually the Germans belong to the twentieth century. Morally, socially and politically they are still in the Middle Ages. That is the reason why they are despised and hated by all foreigners, and why they must suffer for their numerous sins of omission and commission. Purged and purified, they can rise to the level of contemporary civilisation, for progress is the law of social evolution everywhere. The Germans to-day have nothing to give to the world except their books and their inventions; but they must learn a great deal from England, France, Italy, and America before they can call themselves a civilised people.

The most noticeable feature of German society as a whole is the spirit of excessive megalomania that pervades it. This atmosphere poisons the whole life of the nation. The Germans believe that they are the greatest, wisest, bravest, ablest, noblest and best people on earth. They not only believe it but also say so, and proclaim it in their writings and discourses. As a corollary they despise all other peoples as incapable and worthless. Even a noted scientist like Professor Oswald speaks of the Germans as the "chosen people" ("das auserwahlte Volk"). Of course, he cannot tell by whom and for what this people has been "chosen"; but such is the childish vanity of this well-instructed nation. I remember reading this sentence in a book about the future of Germany : "We are the best-educated and the bravest nation in the world." I need not quote from the rabid effusions of the Pan-Germans, with which we are now sufficiently familiar.

I was at first at a loss how to explain that strange declaration of the King of Bavaria at the beginning of the war : "We shall win, whatever may be the number of enemies" ! But I found that every German, high and low, rich and poor, suffers from this curious mental derangement. It is not easy to understand how this psychological condition has arisen. The Germans have no reason to have such a high opinion of themselves. They have not achieved more than the other civilised nations of the world. Their position does not warrant such absurd pride and self-esteem. They have not been the pioneers of human civilisation, like the Egyptians or the Chinese. They have not promulgated great religions, like the Jews, the Arabs, and the Hindus. They have not created the noblest art, philosophy and literature, like the Greeks. They have not discovered and colonised vast continents, like the Spaniards. They have not led the way in founding democratic institutions, like the English and the French. They have not organised wonderful empires, like the English and the Romans. They are not the creators of modern art and literature, like the Italians.

The Germans have also contributed their quota to human culture, but they have not done more than other nations. They cannot even claim to be the first among equals. In fact, they have accomplished less than other ancient and modern nations, though it is of course impossible to compare such different culture-values as Buddhism, Greek sculpture, Beethoven, Shakespeare, and the American Declaration of Independence.

The war of 1870-71 has resulted in the moral suicide of a whole people. At present the Germans are hopelessly materialistic in this respect. They know that they won the victories of 1870-71 and proclaimed the new German Empire at Versailles because they were superior to the French in force. They believe that they owe their present security and prosperity to Moltke, and not to Goethe and Kant. They have learned that Force alone can protect a nation against its enemies. This experience has led them to exaggerate the virtue of Force as a necessary factor in evolution in the present imperfect condition of human society. They have learned a great truth, but they have so distorted and misinterpreted it that it has become a venomous lie in their hands. They have glorified Force and offered incense to this new god, which has rescued them from their Egyptian bondage of past centuries. They have jumped from one extreme to another, as they have forgotten that virtue lies in the mean. They have at last come to know the use of Force, but they are also eager to proceed to its abuse. I was talking at an evening party to Graf X—, and explaining to him the importance of securing the goodwill of the Oriental nations for the German cause, when he suddenly said (in English): "We must hack our way through." A Persian gentleman assured a German diplomat that the Persian people sympathised with Germany! but the latter replied: "Two machine-guns would be more useful than sympathy"! A German journalist said to me: "Everything in this country turns round war and 'soldiering.'" The most favourite toy for German children during the war was the "dicke Bertha" ("fat Bertha"), as the 42-centimetre gun employed by the Germans at the seige of Antwerp was christened. Models of this gun were bought and kept by German families with great piety, like the figure of a tutelary goddess. All Germany seemed to accept it as the greatest emblem of virtue and glory. In Germany the universal faith in Force obtrudes itself on the attention of a foreigner at every step. This war must now teach the Germans that those who take up the sword shall perish by the sword.

The cult of Force has naturally led to dreams of world-conquest. The Germans had developed such excessive political ambition before this war that they aimed at nothing more or less than a "Weltreich." Megalomania and the faith in Force must breed such monstrous progeny. The Germans believed that they could easily defeat England, France, Russia, and the whole world put together. A German official said to me: "What can America do to us?" The remark convinced me that this nation was doomed, as blindness and vanity could not go further. As the German regards all other nations with utter contempt, he draws the necessary conclusion that he must rule over them. A German gentleman, whom I met in a boarding-house in Wiesbaden, said: "We must either win a world-empire, or perish." I said to myself: "The latter alternative is certainly preferable." A German lady, who was more modest than the majority of her countrymen, said: "We must not think that we can defeat England. If we make peace with England, Germany and England can dominate the whole world between them." A Spanish student, who was present, said: "That would be very sad for the whole world, I think." The Germans actually believed that they would crush all their enemies within three months, and celebrate the Christmas of 1914 at home as undisputed masters of Europe! This is not a joke, but a real fact of Germen life, however incredible it may seem to all of us. As the war dragged on, and the pinch of hunger began to be felt, I heard this plaint very often: "We thought that the war would last only three months, or, at the most, half a year. But it has turned out otherwise." In contrast to such fatal folly, which was due to sheer megalomania, we may remember Lord Kitchener's forecast that the war would last three years, though the Germans laughed at this prophecy at the time.

The English knew that they would win the war in the end, but they did not underrate their adversaries, as they had a closer grasp of realities and a better knowledge of the world-situation. The Germans really "ran amok," for they went forth to fight in a fit of madness. During my sojourn in Germany I saw that the whole country was a political Bedlam, and nothing more. I found no trace of wisdom, insight or sound judgment anywhere.

It is a wrong idea that only a certain class or a few statesmen entertained such wild schemes. The Prussian Junker was the first to covet his neighbour's goods, but now the whole nation is infected with such fatuous ambition. I listened to a discussion on the Belgian question in a village public-house near Wiesbaden in January, 1917. The general opinion seemed to be summed up at the end by a middle-aged farmer in these words (spoken in dialect): "Well, if we give up Belgium, all this blood has been shed in vain." A learned professor, who is loved and respected by all his friends for his noble character, said in the spring of 1918: "If this great offensive succeeds, there must be no more talk of evacuating Belgium. All that must be kept. It was part of the old German Empire." A German general, whom I met in a sanatorium in the autumn of 1917, delivered a speech on Hindenburg's birthday, and said : " Belgium is a holy land to us now, as it has been watered by the blood of thousands of our heroic sons. It is foolish to talk of giving it up." These opinions, uttered at wide intervals by representatives of different classes of society, proved to me that German imperialism really menaced Europe with servitude, and converted me to President Wilson's view of the aims and designs of the German Government. But I saw that the whole nation was to blame, and not merely the Government, which executed the will of the people. The German press was unanimous in its approval of the policy of the Government; and even the Socialists voted all the war credits up to the last moment.

The Germans clung to their delusions with desperate tenacity till the final catastrophe. . . . In the summer of 1918 a Berlin professor wrote to a colleague that the people were following with keen anxiety the course of the offensive on the Western front, from which they all hoped for "final victory and a German peace" ("endgultigen Sieg und den deutschen Frieden"). The peculiar phrase, "a German peace," meant that Germany should keep all that she had conquered since August, 1914. This was the cherished aim of all Germans, without distinction of class or party, throughout the war. I know that it was so, whatever the hypocritical politicians may have said in their public speeches.

The Germans think that they are really so superior to other nations that they may regard themselves as beings of a different order altogether. They are the real Men; all others are specimens for zoological museums. They deny the existence of a common bond of humanity between themselves and other peoples, as the gulf between them and the rest of mankind cannot be bridged by such superficial characteristics as an erect posture and other peculiarities of human anatomy. A morbid sense of racial superiority can deaden our finer feelings and blunt our sympathy with our fellow-men.

Some Americans defended slavery on the ground that the negroes really belonged to a different species, and could therefore be treated like animals. The Germans look upon all other nations, European and Oriental, in much the same way. They fancy that they are as superior to the other European nations as these latter are above the semi-civilised Asiatics in the scale of civilisation. As a consequence of this strange aberration the Germans hold themselves bound by no law of humanity in their dealings with other nations. They do not observe the rules and practices enjoined by "international law," for this law has been made by creatures who are no better than animals.

The lords of creation are not to be controlled by such irrelevant enactments ! The Germans have committed the atrocities which have exposed them to the wrath of the entire world because they have learned to despise all men as brutes. This explanation at least deserves careful consideration. They are cruel and brutal towards the conquered, as we are cruel to animals, which we slaughter without remorse or compunction for our advantage. They violate the honour of respectable ladies in occupied territory because they look upon all non-German women only as females. They burn and devastate like the Huns and the Mongols because they have no pity for the sufferings of others. A German lady bewailed the hard lot of her countrymen in the regions now occupied by the armies of the Entente. A friend remarked : "But the German officers have been quartered on the people of Belgium and France during four years." The lady replied : "Well, a German officer, that is a different thing altogether."

A Persian gentleman said to a German lady in Berlin : "I am deeply touched at the sight of the wounded soldiers. Can I do something for them ?" She said : "Why do you feel for them ? You are not a German." This remark revels the depths of moral insensibility to which the Germans have sunk during the last fifty years. Even a woman could not understand why a foreigner pitied wounded German soldiers ! I am sure that this typical German woman was incapable of feeling or showing any sympathy for sick and wounded English, French or Italian soldiers. She could judge the Persian gentleman only by the moral standards in which she herself was trained. I am not inditing a libel on the German people when I assert that they regard all non-Germans as sub-human creatures. I myself was both to believe it at first, but I was compelled to bow to the logic of facts. We think that the Germans are men; but they don't think that we are men. It is desirable and necessary that all Europeans, Americans, Asiatics and Africans should know this fact.

It would not be out of place to mention at his point that I am opposed to German colonisation in Africa and Asia even on a small scale. The Germans are morally unfit to administer colonies, because they do not recognise our common human nature at all. In the colonies the Europeans are absolute masters of the native population. They have weapons, organisation and scientific knowledge, and their will is law. The abuse of their giant strength is fraught with the most terrible consequences to the poor aborigines, who are like children or sheep in the hands of men wielding irresistible power. There is no champion of the natives but the moral law in the soul of the European rulers and settlers. . .

Imperialism has begotten many vices in the German character, but avarice is the ruling passion of the German's soul. Gold is his god in public and private life. In this respect the aims of the State coincide with the tendencies of the individual citizen. All Germans are mad in the pursuit of wealth. They are all in a hurry to amass a fortune. I think that this trait explains why the Germans are unpopular in other countries. All men, everywhere, wish to earn money, and it is a duty to work honestly for economic gain. But the Germans are very mean, avaricious, stingy, unscrupulous and selfish. Every foreigner is struck with this characteristic of all Germans without distinction of class. Stones may yield oil, but no generous action can be expected from a German. If he can save a shilling by sponging on others or abusing their confidence, he will surely do so. He has the very disgusting habit of enjoying hospitality without thinking of returning it. He is very willing to eat your cakes, but he cannot waste his own cakes on you. I made the acquaintance of a distinguished German scholar, whom I also agreed to help in his literary work. I presented him with two boxes of good cigars, and tried to win his friendly sympathy in other ways. I used to visit him almost every afternoon. He never offered me a cup of tea, though he had received my gifts and was always very affable and talkative. I noticed that he had his afternoon tea just before I called. It never occurred to him that he should at least once or twice ask me to drink a cup of tea with him. He did not consider it safe even to mention it, as the experiment was too risky. Supposing I had actually accepted the invitation ! It would have meant an economic catastrophe for him. Some German politicians visited Constantinople and invited a few Turkish politicians to see them.

It is reported that they did not offer even a cup of coffee to the Turkish colleagues because, of course, a cup of coffee costs a penny, and the German cannot make such a sacrifice. Such melancholy meanness throws some light on the real character of the average German. A Swedish journalist related how the German guests at a party took away all the cigars. I have forgotten the details of the story, but he ended with these words : "An Englishman never does this sort of thing." The Germans have really a genius for petty selfishness of this kind. It is impossible for a German to make friends. He is an anti-social, egotistic and unlovable creature. At present he is interested chiefly in money. A German gentleman said to me : "This time France must pay us an indemnity of 45 milliards. We took too little in 1871." I mentioned to a professor of philosophy the news that the Bolshevik Government had delivered to the German officials the first instalments of the indemnity in gold bars. He asked me to read the newspaper to him and said : "What does it say? Have the gold bars been actually delivered?" I replied : "Yes. They have been deposited in the Reichsbank." The exponent of philosophy gave a grunt of satisfaction at this news, and I could see that he was trying to visualise the glittering bars of gold which Germany had gained as booty. Avarice has corroded the soul of this nation and made it unfit for the common offices of courtesy and friendship. I don't know how it can be cured of this vice.

While the Germans threaten the whole world with conquest and "Kultur," their social and political institutions at home are of the mediaeval and reactionary type. Slaves are proper instruments for enslaving others. Despotism, bureaucracy and caste are the foundations of German society. When I was there the air reeked with servility and snobbery. Those who had lived in England, France, America or Switzerland found life in Germany altogether insupportable. The worship of the Kaiser was the creed of half Germany. Fulsome flattery of the monarch was considered a mark of patriotism, and reminded me of the age of the Tudors. The bust of the Kaiser was a pestilential nuisance in Berlin. It was crowned with wreaths and flowers in the big concert house in Mauerstrasse, like the statue of a heathen god. I entered a chemist's shop, and there it was on the shelf, with its repellent expression of insolent braggadocio. Go where you would you could not escape this ubiquitous bust. The royal family was also on sale in pictures and cards of all sorts.

The Empress, the Crown Prince, his children, their cousins, their nurses and the relatives of the nurses were all very much in evidence in the bookshops and at the street corners. The whole show was very disgusting and ludicrous. But it was an important social institution of Germany. Let us hope that the Germans have now got rid of the Hohenzollerns for ever. The monarchy may be abolished, but German society cannot be freed so easily from bureaucracy and the spirit of caste. In Germany everything is done for the people, and nothing by the people. As there are no democratic institutions, the functionaries fear no control or criticism. They meddle with everything, and plague the people in a thousand different ways. All Germans who have lived for some time in England or America refuse to return to their native land. They have breathed the free atmosphere of English and American society, and detest the bureaucratic system of Germany. I met a German merchant who had lived for more than ten years in England. We were at the dinner table in a sanatorium at Partenkirchen, in Bavaria.

The talk turned on the merits and demerits of the English people. A patriotic German lady said : "The French are our old enemies. But why have the English joined them? They are a gang of robbers." I remained silent. The merchant replied : "But England has much better political institutions. There, in London, I am I" ("Ich bin ich"), "but here . . . . " At this point he put both his hands on his ears as the most effective method of expressing what he meant. That phrase, "Ich bin ich", sums up centuries of English history. It is curious that the uneducated merchant could find no other words to pay his tribute of praise for English freedom. In the summer of 1917 a lady wrote to me from Berlin : "All our rights are being taken away. It is a miserable time here." The Junker class had established a reign of terror in order to stifle adverse criticism. Many Liberals and Socialists were in "Schutzhaft" during the war.

The Germans seemed to be quite unconscious of their slavery. They had known only this system in their lives. A German journalist said to me : "What do you mean by talking of free America? We have as much freedom here as the Americans." I tried to explain to him the difference between German and American institutions; but he did not see the point. Another German friend said : "You must be born a German in order to understand our system." I thanked my stars that I was not born a German. Germany is several centuries behind the other European countries in social evolution. This was is perhaps the beginning of the end of the old system.

The spirit of caste is more prevalent in German society than in other countries. Every man must have his "Titel," which is always prefixed to his name. It would be very impolite to omit the "Titel" in writing or speaking to a person. Thus it often happens that a man's name is never heard in conversation. He is always "Herr Professor," or "Herr Postdirektor," or "Herr Geheimrat," or even "Herr Baumeister." The mania for a " Titel" goes so far that some people coin curious titles indicating their social position, like "Herr Brauerei-Besitzer" ("Mr. Brewery-Owner"). The enormous number of "Rats" of different species in German society spread the plague of snobbery and servility. Thus there are Geheimrats, Kommerzienrats, Hofrats, etc., etc. A woman will put the husband's title before her name, and call herself "Hofratsgattin" (a Hofrat's wife). One comes across such names as "Lawyer's-widow Mrs. Meyer." A lady chose to call herself "Baron's-mother-in-law Mrs. So-and-So." The spirit of caste leads to strange freaks, which sometimes show bad taste. A learned professor dedicated his book to his wife, but added "Baron's-widow" to her name, as she had married a baron before our lucky professor won her heart and her money. Society must know that the professor's wife was no ordinary person but a Baron's widow ! Germany needs a breath of Democracy in order to disperse these miasmic vapours of mediaeval feudalism which choke her spirit and smother her moral life. It is to be hoped that caste will also relax its hold on German society after the expulsion of the Hohenzollerns and the establishment of democratic institutions.

The history of Germany during the last fifty years may be described as the tragedy of a whole society. This nation is utterly sick in head and heart. It has lost its wits, and it has killed its conscience. "Whom the gods destroy, they first make mad." It will take a very long time to restore this demented and demoralised people to health and sanity.

It is a great day in a young man's life when he first sees one of the ancient historic cities of the world, such as Rome, Athens, Benares or Constantinople. As I walked up the street leading from the railway station to the hotel in Stamboul my mind was in an ecstasy of delight and wonder. It was not what I saw, but what I thought of, that worked like magic in the brain. To a student of history Constantinople (which, fortunately, preserves its Greek name, in spite of the unspeakable

Turk,) is a place of pilgrimage. Of course, the joy at the fulfilment of a long-cherised dream was mixed with deep sadness at the fate of the city, from which the scholars had gone forth to Italy with the balm of Greek learning for the sick and weary mediaeval world. But it was well that I could see it, even in its misery and degradation. The Turk will pass away, so said I, but the glory of this city will remain. Sooner or later it will be restored to its only rightful claimants, the Hellenes, whose name it bears. In the meantime I might learn what life here has to teach me.

It was in the spring and summer of 1915, when the loveliness of Nature stood in strange contrast to the carnage on the battlefields of Gallipoli. The Bosphorus, perhaps the most beautiful spot on earth, was a haven of calm and peace in the midst of this warring world of brute force and more brutish intrigue. But it was my business to watch the operation of political forces and to meet all types of characters in the course of the daily routine, for I was supposed to carry on political propaganda. I should have liked to live on the Bosphorus as a poet or a painter; but, as I was neither the one nor the other, I had to make the best of the situation and figure as "a politician." I shall write about the chief lessons that I learned during my six months' sojourn in that Dar-i-Saadat, the seat of the Caliphate. I trust that all Orientals, and especially the Muslims of India and Egypt, will ponder well the meaning of my words.

I shall begin with the Turks. And the first thing I have to say is that the Turks, as a nation, are utterly unfit to assume the leadership of the Muslim world. They have been, and are, only a predatory tribe, without culture and political capacity. It was an evil day for the Muhammadan world when the Turk was entrusted with the Caliphate. The Turks have no brains; that is the plain truth. They can fight well, but they cannot administer or organise. They have been in possession of a vast empire for several centuries; but they have no great or noble national literature. All nations have produced great literature as the spiritual sign and symbol of their political ascendancy.

Athens, Rome, Spain, Portugal, Elizabethan England and Vikram's India are now more familiar to us through the names of Aeschylus, Sophocles, Virgil, Calderon, Camoens, Shakespeare and Kalidasa than those of the statesmen and warriors who flourished during the during the periods of their political expansion. Political success has always led to the complete self-expression of a gifted nation in literature, art and philosophy. But we look in vain for these fruits of empire in Turkey.

The Turks could not sing of speculate, as they are really very low in the scale of mental evolution. Nature has not endowed them with brains. They have also been the rulers of Greece; but they have learned nothing from their subjects, whose language is the key to the highest wisdom and culture. The Romans were also rude barbarians when they conquered Greece. But they yielded to the spell of Greek genius, and "conquered Greece conquered her conquerors," as the Roman poet truly declared. Rome produced great poets and thinkers under the tutelage of Greece, but the Turkish mind has been a barren soil which has brought forth nothing but the thorns and thistles of superstition and ribaldry. History has clearly demonstrated that the Turk has no intellectual potentialities. He is therefore really unfit for leadership of any kind, as a leader is distinguished by his intellectual pre-eminence over his colleagues. How can such gifted peoples as the Egyptians and the Indians follow the guidance of the uncivilised and uncivilisable Turk? The Turk cannot guide; he is absolutely incompetent and helpless on account of his mental inferiority. An Egyptian gentleman, speaking of the Turks, said; "They know only two things, war and mosques." This is the opinion of a cultivated Muslim, who has lived about six years in Turkey. Another Muslim journalist said to me : "The Turks are the little brothers of the Prussians; they are stupid and arrogant."

Further, the Turks cannot administer or organise. Turkey has become the by-word of the modern age, because Turkish rule has been characterised by the grossest corruption, oppression and disorder. I speak of Turkish rule in countries inhabited chiefly by Muslims. Self-indulgence and indolence are the principal aims of the Turkish magnate. The Turks cannot govern little Syria well : how can they help other Muhammadans to acquire the capacity of self-government ? I once asked a Muslim physician in Berlin: "Why is there such misrule in Syria ? Can't the Turkish Government organise an efficient police force ?" He replied : "Yes; but the chief of police will himself join the robbers and highwaymen of the country !" I then understood that it was really a hopeless case of degeneracy. Another Muslim politician, in the course of a discussion, said : "Yes, Syria is a very rich country; but the organisation of government—" and here he stopped short, as he did not wish to criticise the Ottoman Government adversely. But his sudden silence was more eloquent than any words could be. There was a painful pause, till I turned the conversation to other topics.

As the Turks are a barbarous tribe, the Muslims of India and Egypt make a great mistake in identifying their cause with the fortunes of the Ottomans. The Turks have repeatedly given proof of their brutality and depravity by organising massacres of peaceful Armenian and Greek populations and violating hundreds of Greek women, even with the sanction of the police authorities. If this be Islam, I should blush for the faith of 70,000,000 of my Indian fellow-citizens. The civilised Muslims of India and Egypt lose immensely in the estimation of the Western world by associating with this semi-savage horde. Europe is free from religious fanaticism at present; but Europe and America will "always be at war with Ottomanism," as President Taft has well said. If the Muslims of India wish to appear in company with their Hindu brethren on the public platforms of the civilised world, they must first wash their hands clean of Ottomanism in all its shapes and disguises. The Turkish system of ruling by massacre and rape is neither Islamic nor rational; it is pure, unadulterated Ottoman savagery, worthy of Chengiz Khan and Halaku. We cannot make common cause with such marauders simply because they live east of Suez and profess Islam. The Muslims of India and

Egypt must realise their own privileged position, and disclaim all connection with Central Asian freebooters.

During my stay in Constantinople I learned that the Turks have no real sympathy with other Muslim nations. They are not Pan-Islamists; they are Ottoman nationalists. But they wish to exploit and use other Muslim peoples for their own purposes with the cry of Pan-Islamism. Pan-Islamism is one of the most curious farces of the last decade. It simply means that other Muslim nations should sing the praises of the Turk and acknowledge his overlordship, and a few adventurers and charlatans from every Muslim land should swagger about in Stamboul on an allowance of £10 to £50 a month from the Turkish Government. This was all I could discover of the famous Pan-Islamic movement, which was supposed to be paving the way for the unification and revival of Islam under the leadership of the pious hero, Enver Pasha.

The Turks care only for their own tribe; they have no interest in the affairs or destinies of the millions of Muslims scattered in all parts of the world, from Java to Senegal. They must set their own house in order, and their policy is quite sound. They know that it is impossible to embody the spiritual unity of Islam in an external political institution embracing all the Muslims of the world. This fantastic idea finds no favour among Turkish patriotic circles. But they do not frankly say so. They think that they can gain some sympathy (and sometimes money, too) by posing as the leaders of Islam, the custodians of the holy places, and the heirs of the traditions of the Caliphate. They pay a few pounds a month to several Indian, Egyptian, Algerian, Tunisian, Sudanese, and other Muslim enthusiasts to carry on Pan-Islamic propaganda for the glory of Turkey and the ministers of the Young Turk party. But they are not prepared to make any sacrifices for the common cause. If they get something as high priests of Pan-Islamism, well and good; but they will not risk anything for the sake of the other Muslim peoples.

The Muslims of India and Egypt must realise that they worship a false idol when they waste their sympathies on

Turkey as the head of Islam. Of couise, the Turks were very glad to pocket a few lakhs of Indian money during the Balkan wars; and they sent a holy (or ordinary) carpet with a message of thanks, which did not cost much. But there are millions of starving Muslim labourers in India who could have been helped with this money. We should know that charity begins at home. But it is the fashion of some Muslims to be enthusiastic about everything out of India, and to remain indifferent to the claims and needs of their co-religionists at home. Such an attitude is fostered by the hollow cant of Islamism. I have been at the heart and centre of Islam, in the innermost court of the shrine of Pan-Islamism; and I declare that it is all a fraud and a hoax, designed to impose upon credulous Muslims in distant lands.

The Turks are very unpopular among all free Muslims. The only Muslims who swear by them seem to be those waifs and strays who have no country of their own. The Turks shown themselves to be cruel, selfish, and arrogant. It is impossible to work with them. The most significant commentary on the Jihad proclaimed by the Turks has been furnished by the revolt of the Arabian tribes against Ottoman rule. If the Turks were really faithful Pan-Islamists and worthy succesors of the Caliphs, why should the pious Arabs try to overthrow Turkish rule in Arabia and Syria with the aid of the English, who are non-Muslims ? This fact must open the eyes of all Muslims to the true situation.

The Turks have even attempted to suppress the Arabic tongue in their dominions, as they have pursued the "patriotic" policy of "Ottomanising" all their subjects in language and thus securing uniformity in their much-divided empire. But the folly of such experiments is obvious, as the small, unlettered tribe cannot assimilate the numerous and cultured Arab nation. The Turks have thus no special claim on the sympathy of other Muslim patriots on the ground of "Pan-Islamic" interests. There is no such thing as Pan-Islamism. Nationalism is a living force in Persia, Arabia, Egypt, Turkey and Afghanistan. The Turks wish to stifle the national sentiment of the Eyptians and the Arabs, while they try every means of keeping Ottoman patriotism alive ! Such is their boasted love of Islam. A Persian gentleman said to me : "These Turks are great humbugs. They wish that we should bow to them and serve their interests in the name of the Caliphate." For some time there was a big tempest in the teapot of Egyptian nationalism in Turkey. Some leaders proposed that the Egyptians should take up a Pan-Islamic position and lose their national identity as subjects of the Caliphate. Other more enlightened leaders opposed this mediaeval policy and stood up for the traditions of the Egyptian National Party, which had adopted the motto : Egypt for the Egyptians.'' These were buttons bearing the device of the Egyptian National Party (in addition to the Ottoman symbols); and this practice exposed them to the wrath of some Turkish ministers, as I heard from a reliable source. The pure "Nationalists" branded the other group as mercenaries, who had sold themselves to Turkey. This taunt seemed to derive further justification from the fact that most "Pan-Islamists" have been in the pay of the Turkish Government. The "Pan-Islamists" retorted by stigmatising the Nationalists as infidels and thoughtless visionaries, who played into the hands of the English. The Turkish Government was even reported to have withdrawn its financial assistance from some Egyptian Nationalist leaders in Berlin, who found themselves in difficult circumstances on account of the exigencies of the war.

The Turks did not like the national propaganda of the sincere Egyptian patriots, who insisted that Egypt was not a part of Turkey but an independent nation. The "Pan-Islamist" party had, of course, more money at its disposal and started a monthly Journal in Berlin. But the majority of the contributors were always Germans, literary hacks, as far as I could see. This proved that the pro-Turkish group kept up an artificial existence bolstered with Turkish gold, but that the ablest Muslims held aloof from this mischieous movement.

An Egyptian physician once said to me : "You must not confound us with the Turks. We have nothing in common with them except religion. We are an entirely different people." There was much anxiety and trepidation among Egyptian patriots when it was known that the Turks were preparing an an expedition against Egypt. Ottoman ambition ran high in the first year of the war. Every Turkish general compared himself to Saladin and Tarik. I heard that Djemal Pasha, who was in charge of the projected Egyptian had expedition uttered this heroic sentiment: "I will conquer Egypt, or die." I remarked: Well, we shall be very sorry to mourn his loss." The Egyptians were full of fears and misgivings. Egypt had had enough experience of Turkish inroads in the past. An Egyptian leader said to his colleague: "Les Turcs mangeront l'Egypte" ("The Turks will eat up Egypt"). The other replied, in a fit of Pan-Islamic fervour: Qu'ils mangent" ("Let them do so"). But, on second thoughts, he admitted that a Turkish invasions would be a great misfortune for his fertile country. Such is the real opinion of enlightened Muslims about the Turks. It is also the opinion of the entire civilised world.

It is an open secret that there is no love lost between the Turks and the Persians. During the war it was reported that Germany was frequently asked to act as arbitrator in disputes. The Turkish troops levied heavy contributions on the Persian towns which they occupied for some time in the early period of the war. The Turkish official reports spoke of the occupied Persian territory as "conquered regions" ("mama-lik-i-maftuha"). This circumstance embittered the Persian Nationalists and revealed the real psychology of these self-styled friends of Islam. I heard that the Turks were hated by the population of the Persian provinces, which temporarily fell into their hands. It was the same old story of rapine, violence, and cruetly every where. The persians came to the conclusion that the Turk was unteachable, and so he is.

I have come across several pathetic instances of waste of energy and enthusiasm due to the illusions of Pan-Islamism. A young man from Bombay, who had been an engineer in India, come to Turkey in order to take part in the "Holy War," as the law enjoined. He is a sincere and honest

Muslim. He distributed all his money among the poor, and went forth with the Turkish soldiers into the Sinai desert to strike a blow for the faith. His consistent idealism elicited the admiration of all his friends (who, however, did not follow his example). Our knight-errant fell ill and had to return to Damascus. He then discovered that the realities of Ottoman administration did not agree exactly with the dreams of ardent Pan-Islamists. No one cared for him as he lay sick in a small hotel in Damascus. He had given away all his hard-earned savings before donning his armour, but now the Caliphate did not help him in his distress.

The sick hero was rescued from his woeful plight by some Hindu patriots, who heard about him from his friends in Constantinople. They immediately wired him money and asked him to join them after recovery—surely "a sadder and a wiser man." I wonder what this intelligent Muslim now thinks of the "Caliphate." I know several hot "Pan-Islamists" who refused to be naturalised as Ottoman subjects, as they were afraid of being called upon to fight for the holy cause ! They are willing to spend their breath, but cannot do the first duty of a zealous "Pan-Islamist. Of such calibre are some noisy fanatics made ! The Indians resident in Turkey are generally wanderers or adventurers, who are not held in high esteem. A few old men live in the "takiya" (the poor-house). Some of them have married Turkish wives and speak Hindi mixed up with Turkish. They have lost touch with the Mother Country. They are almost always quarrelling among themselves from jealousy and selfishness. The Turkish Government has set selfishness. The Turkish Government has set apart a few pounds a month for Indian propagandists; and there is a general scramble for this prize of indolent charlatanism. Invitations to dinner at the houses of some influential Turks also furnish an occasion for explosions of personal jealousy and uncharitableness. Nothing can be hoped for from this set. They will stew in their own juice for some time, till they are replaced by other Indian fugitives and sturdy vagabonds, who roam about in all Islamic lands.

I learned one lesson in Constantinople which I shall not easily forget. I have learned that good administration is a very rare thing in Asia. I could judge of the merits and demerits of Turkish rule by examining the state of affairs in Stamboul and its neighbourhood. Poverty broods over the whole place. Several quarters of the city present a shapeless mass of charred ruins, as they have not been rebuilt after a conflagration. I thought of San Francisco as I saw these tokens of Turkish lethargy and incompetence. No official is ever in a hurry to finish his work. Every little thing takes an interminably long time. It is the reign of "Yavash! Yavash!" (gently! gently!) I had the melancholy satisfaction of witnessing one of the big fires which are a regular feature of Constantinople life.

The fire blazed away for ten hours. The small wooden houses of the poor were consumed and reduced to cinders in one street after another. The unlucky denizens fled into the big bazaar with bundles under their arms or small boxes on their shoulders—perhaps their entire earthly belongings. But what was the Government doing ? I saw a few ragged policemen and firemen runing along the street several hours after the reddening sky had announced the danger to the whole town. This rabble of official rescuers was manipulating some antiquated apparatus and pouring a thin stream of water on the roaring sea of flames. It was a spectacle which was tragic and ludicrous at the same time. At last the fire abated; but I believe that it was due more to Nature than to the exertions of the Imperial Ottoman Government. I heard that conditions were still worse in the interior of the country. A patriotic Indian gentleman expressed this opinion as the outcome of his experiences of travel in Turkey : "After two years, I have come to the conclusion that the country should be annexed by some European Power!" And this gentleman is a sincere opponent of European imperialism in general.

But he apparently thought that even European conquest was preferable in the interests of the people to Turkish "self-government." I was touched with deep pity as I saw the ranks of Turkish soldiers marching past in the streets of Stamboul and Pera day after day in that eventful summer. These ignorant peasants and working men were torn from their homes and turned into food for cannon to gratify the ambition of a small class of Pashas and Beys, who had lived for generations on the plunder of subjugated countries. I noticed that Enver Pasha was reported in the papers to be always present at the weekly Selamlik, whether from piety or policy I could not judge. These demoralised bourgeois classes were trading on the religious idealism of a brave peasantry! I learned that more than half a million Turkish soldiers were slain on the peninsula of Gallipoli; but I believe that the ministers who drove them to the shambles are still living. They have fled from their country after having ruined it in their folly.

The ambition of Turkish imperialists has laid Turkey in the dust. It was not necessary for Turkey to join the war as an enemy of England. The Entente was always ready even to grant important concessions to Turkey at the outbreak of the war. But the criminal stupidity of a few swashbucklers, who had been educated in Germany, has brought this disaster on the Turkish people. This is the last sad consequence of inefficient administration. A land governed by fools cannot prosper.

The Muslims of India, Egypt, Java and Persia should learn that they must look after the affairs of their own countries in a practical spirit instead of dreaming of the Caliphate. There is nothing but dirt, and dead dogs, and scheming rascals in Stamboul. It is only distance that lends enchantment to the view in this case. Each Muslim nation should organise itself, and also, of course, sympathise with other Muslim countries. But every Muslim's duty lies at home, in the corner of the world where he is born.

"The old order changeth, yielding place to new." The Caliphate has had its day. The stream of history does not flow backward. Islam, as a religion, cannot be bound up with any particular theory of political organisation. We live in the twentieth century of the Christian era, not in the eighth. The Muslims should get rid of these mediaeval rags—the Caliphate and the Jihad. Islam, too, will pass away, for the world moves forward and will not wait for Islam or Hinduism or Buddhism. The Muslims should modernise themselves and learn the new ideas and ideals of the Western world. The vanguard of humanity to-day is in Europe and America, not in Arabia, Mesopotamia or Tibet. A new heaven and a new earth will be fashioned in the future, but not out of the debris of outworn creeds and formulae. The educated Muslims should take the lead in assimilating modern modes of thought. This is not the time to live and die by dispensations which were great and new forces centuries ago. Prophets may come and prophets may go, but Humanity goes on for ever in its pursuit of truth and virtue. The Muslims should also advance with the times, and must not "attempt the future's portals with the past's blood-rusted key."

The sad fate of the Turkish people proves that there is no magic in national "self-government" as such. It all depends on the character and capacity of the governing class, for the peasants and the working men cannot take part in the administration. They pay taxes, and expect to receive the benefits of a sound administration in return. The upper and middle classes of Egypt, India and Persia cannot administer successfully without European control and guidance. They are wanting in energy, public spirit and technical knowledge. They can neither organise the defence of the country nor establish a good system of internal government. A mixed European and Oriental administration is the best for these countries, as the European officials are honest, energetic and capable, while the Orientals know the customs and traditions of the people. There is no harm in admitting that the upper and middle classes of Asia are not fit for all the tasks of progressive administration in this age.

The Turkish Government had to employ European engineers for the Hedjaz railway. The Persians invited an American to put their finances in order, and paid Swedish officers to organise a police force for them. Such a mixed administration already exists in countries which form part of the British and the French colonial empires, though the European element is perhaps unnecessarily large and the Oriental colleagues are not given their due. These are minor faults, but the principle of the mixed personnel is sound. Among European nations, England has been already in the field for a century, and France has also acquired vast dependencies in Asia and Africa. It is, therefore, wise to co-operate with these nations for the establishment and continuance of good government in Asiatic countries, whatever colour the flag may have.

The interests of the peasants and working men of Asia require peace, order, justice, education, organisation, and permanent contact with Europe and America. A purely national administration in an Oriental country, composed of the effeminate sons of the landowners, lawyers, bankers, manufacturers, priests and other parasitic classes, cannot secure these blessings for the people. They must be trained, controlled and inspired by European officials, or worse than Turkish disorder would ensue. The people of Asiatic countries cannot pay the high price of perpetual misrule and stagnation for the satisfaction of seeing a national flag float over the public buildings of the capital. For purposes of external defence, co-operation between Englishmen and the Indians or the Egyptians is also imperatively necessary. Egypt, Persia and India would be again overrun by barbarians if England were to withdraw from Asia, as the Britons were enslaved by the Teutons as soon as the Roman garrisons left the country.

It is, therefore, necessary to readjust our views to the actual circumstances of the situation as this war has revealed them to us. We should think of the British (and the French) Empires as single political units, which must be preserved in their integrity for a long time to come. We must fight for the defence of these States against external invasion, for the dissolution of these Empires can result only in a change of masters for us. At the same time, we should try to educate and elevate the people by teaching them to appreciate English and French ideals and setting on foot popular movements for the extension of democratic institutions in Asia and Africa. "Self-government" under a purely Oriental governing class would be no blessing for the peasants and the working men, and would finally lead to conquest by some European power. The system of mixed administration seems to be the only natural and necessary solution of the problem. Then the fires in Constantinople would be extinguished promptly and effectively by trained firemen working under European leadership. And that is what the people of Asia ask for.

Oriental life in Berlin during the war was quite picturesque and many-sided. But it was something of a tragedy, as I shall have occasion to show in the sequel. There were all nations of the East in the streets of Berlin: conceited Young Turks, fussy Egyptians, acute but pessimistic Persians, nondescript Arabs, handsome Geórgians and others, who fancied that the triumph of German arms would redress the wrongs of their countries. Berlin was the Mecca of Oriental patriots of all shades of opinion. Their common bond was hatred of England and France. Every one formed plans for the regeneration of his Fatherland after the war. Their optimism was rather premature, as the ruthless logic of events has demonstrated. But during the first two years of the war these Oriental nationalists were elated with high hopes and went about in a state of political intoxication produced by a too ample dose of the Pan-Germanic "hasheesh." Thus a noted middle-aged Egyptian Politician said on one occasion : "The liberation of Egypt is certain. I am 100 per cent sure of it." A party of young Egyptian students met in solemn conclave one day to discuss the measures to be taken immediately after the end of the war ! It is worth remembering as a joke of the wartime that some Egyptian politicians had even nominated themselves in imagination to the highest offices of state in free Egypt ! The Turks were all chauvinistic, and it was their habit to decry other Islamic nations. Thus a young Turkish official said to me : "You know it is pure Turkish blood, Anatolian blood, that has been shed at Gallipoli. We Turks have thus saved the cause of

Islam. Others have done nothing. We pity poor India and the Indian people."

The supercilious tone of these remarks well illustrates the spirit of the new Turkish imperialists. Some Algerians also carried on their "propaganda" in bad French. One of them delivered a public lecture, which was insufferably dull, and which really proved that the people of Algeria were not discontented with French rule. But the obtuse patriot could not see the point. Unbounded optimism and sincere faith in the power and professions of Germany were common to all these Oriental "Nationalists." As I contemplated their somewhat sad countenances and heard their plaintive accents, I was touched with pity, as I knew that they sighed for an irrevocable past. They talked of the "Caliphate," of the age of the Crusades, of the Jihad-i-Akbar ! I could not tell them all I thought. They were the rearguard of a vanishing host, not the pioneers of a new generation. They fed themselves on words, words, words. And they rejoiced at the German victories, as if they could sustain themselves by vicarious strength. And at last that bubble, too, burst !

There were influences at work which began to mar the joy and weaken the self-confidence of this carnival of hope. As usual, these Muslim patriots and Pan-Islamists could not get on with the Prussians. No one can get on with the Prussians. It is, of course, dangerous to deal in general maxims; but I give a safe rule for all Orientals to follow : "Never have anything to do with a Prussian."

The chances are that you will rue your folly if you disregard this precept. These Orientals, thus gathered together in Berlin soon found out that they lived in a society of snobs, bullies, boors, churls and cads. An Arab gentleman was once heard to say, "The English are at least gentlemen," and this utterance was reported against him. A Turkish journalist arrived one day in high glee, visited some Prussians, and left for Constantinople the same evening ! He had had enough of Germany and the Germans in the course of twelve hours. Some rude affront or arrogant phrase had revealed the true Prussian to him, and he was disgusted and disheartened beyond measure. As Egyptian patriot, who was an enthusiastic admirer of the Germans before he came to Berlin, at last uttered this remarkable sentiment : "When peace comes, I shall leave this country the same evening without waiting to take my luggage with me !" On other occasions he would grumble and say, "They treat us like dogs." He also related to me that a high Egyptian official, who was invited to Berlin, left with this commentary on the situation : "They play with us like children. Do they think I am a boy?" A Persian gentleman was once talking to me of his future plans of work. I said, in a tone of banter, "Well, you will surely marry a pretty German girl, and settle in this country." To my surprise, he said : "Je n'aime pas les Allemands" ("I do not like the Germans"). We spoke French on this occasion. I did not pursue the conversation further. If I had asked him, he would undoubtedly have told me his story. There is a world of meaning in that short and pithy remark : "Je n'aime pas les Allemands." The reason is not far to seek.

The Prussians are a selfish, rude, and arrogant people. They look upon themselves as demi-gods, as veritable super-men. They suffer from incurable megalomania. Their success in the war of 1870-71 has turned their heads. They believe that they are the greatest nation on earth, and that all others are miserable worms and mannikins. They are not bound to show courtesy to inferior creatures. They must teach these Orientals that they are not the equals of the divine German race. The German is born to rule, and all others to serve. This inordinate pride must estrange all friends and alienate the sympathies of colleagues and fellow-workers. The course of events has in this case proved the wisdom of the old saying : "Pride goeth before destruction, a haughty spirit before a fall." The Germans could not win over the Orientals in Berlin because their frog-in-the-well pride robbed them of manners.

The Orientals are noted for their politeness, which they even carry to excess. But the German are extremely deficient in this common virtue. Courtesy is the lubricant of social life, and the absence of it in German society naturally led to continual friction. I know of no Oriental who left Berlin with feelings of esteem and friendship for the Germans. I used to laugh and say : "If you want to make a man anti-German, send him to Berlin." It was a most curious and instructive phenomenon. All persons who have lived in Paris or London love France and England ever afterwards. They have pleasant memories of their sojourn among cultivated and sociable gentlemen. But every foreigner who spends some time in Prussia feels as if he were living in a menagerie. He meets only with insults and rebuffs on all sides; he is robbed, over-reached, and exploited by every one whom he encounters. These Oriental patriots were not by any means peculiarly unfortunate in their experiences. A Spanish gentleman expressed this opinion in the presence of several Germans : "I admire Germany as a powerful State; but I don't like the individual Germans" ("aber die einzelnen Deutschen liebe ich nicht"). He related to me how he had to suffer at the hands of these unscrupulous, greedy, and intolerable Berlin people during his stay in Germany. I am sure that that young Spaniard will never say a good word for Germany in his life. The same result was produced by similar circumstances in the case of the Orientals who flocked to Berlin in such a devout spirit in the first year of the war. That was surely a sad disappointment. But worse was to follow.

Want of manners is not the only fault through which the Germans have lost the sympathy of the Oriental representatives in Berlin. There are other vices in the German character which have made personal confidence and co-operation impossible. I generalise from numerous single incidents, as I have been an amused spectator of many a tragi-comic affair in this little Oriental world, this "Asia Minor" of Berlin. The root of the whole trouble is that the Germans have no character. They are a mean and dishonourable people; in fact, they are singularly devoid of the sense of honour. They work hard, and are patriotic, but that is perhaps their only virtue. Their best and best-educated men tell lies and break their promises in the most important affairs of life. They seem to think that they are really "above good and evil," if one may judge from the nonchalant spirit in which they deal with questions involving the gravest consequences to others. They never think of the other persons, always of themselves. Self is their god, and they have no regard for anybody where their interests or even their whims are concerned. Now this trait in the German character must make all co-operation impossible. Society. Society is based on truth and mutual regard. If a man in authority is known to be unreliable, the State, which he represents, must fail in its plans and enterprises, as no one will work for or with him for a long time. The Germans can never inspire confidence in others, for they are a dishonourable people. They will injure others without remorse or compunction in order to serve their interests even in small matters. Thus a distinguished scholar was prevented from leaving **Berlin** for Constantinople, presumably because some petty subaltern wished to exploit him in Berlin. Of course, that man has a grievance against Germany. A gentleman was asked to come all the way from the United States at considerable personal sacrifice to himself; but he was left in the lurch after his arrival in Europe because the little Prussian despot of the office had changed his mind. An energetic Oriental gentleman was requested to undertake some very important work in a neutral country; but he found that the German had not fulfilled his part of the bargain, and he was in a difficult and even dangerous situation for some time. A noted Egyptian leader was at first asked to write an article for a semi-official paper; but the German editor refused to publish it or to return it to him after he had spent much time and money on it ! He was told that his article had been disposed of in a proper manner ! When he asked me how I explained such absurd tomfoolery, I said : "How can I tell you ? I am not a German." These are small matters constitute the business of life everywhere. And character is often revealed in small affairs.

But the Germans have displayed the same disregard for truth and fair-play in very serious matters, in which the lives and fortunes of their friends were at stake. Such consistent and invariable meanness is suicidal, and to-day one may say that Germany has not a single friend in Asia. On this occasion I confine my remarks to the daily happenings in the piebald, polyglot circle in Berlin, which I actually frequented for a long time. In fact, the unaccountably mean ways of the Germans formed a staple subject of conversation among the Orientals. There was always some scandal going on. It was not a question of personalities. It was always the same, whoever the parties concerned happened to be. Every one complained, sooner or later, that he had been exploited, or deceived, or otherwise ill-treated by some German with whom he had to deal. I at first thought that these accusations could not be taken seriously, as misunderstandings often arise in the course of affairs, and these Oriental might possibly be vain and sensitive young men. But I was led to inquire further, when the cases multiplied with lapse of time. I noticed that Oriental gentlemen of the most diverse types of character had the same thing to say. . .

With regard to the Indian Nationalists in Berlin, I observed that the greater part of their time and energy was spent in quarrelling among themselves and telling lies against one another. They had not much work; and idle hands always find mischief to do. Some of the leading members came from words to blows on one occasion, and each party averred that the other had commenced the attack. Such a combination of pugilistic and "patriotic" activity caused quite a scandal in Berlin. One of them went about slandering his colleagues everywhere, and told his German and Oriental acquaintances that the other Indians were thieves, swindlers and impostors. These gentlemen were supposed to be members of an association, or "Gesellschaft"; but they could never work together harmoniously I had no direct knowledge of the corporate activities of this association after the winter of 1915-16; but I learned something now and then from the conversation and correspondence of a few friends. There were all kinds of people in that association : sincere but misguided patriots, unprincipled adventurers, self-indulgent parasites, scheming notoriety hunters, simple-minded students, and some victims of circumstance.

The number was never very large. Some pamphlets were written, and some foolish intrigues were set on foot. On the whole, the group made a very unfavourable impression on Berlin society on account of its perpetual quarrels and splits. The Germans also paid money for their own selfish purposes, but they had no respect for such needy "patriots." Some of the members tried to ingratiate themselves with the German officials by acting as mercenary German agents and meddling with matters which were not related in any way to the Indian movement. There was much hobnobbing with Irishmen, Egyptians and other anti-English agitators. But nothing came out of it. A deputation visited Constantinople, but could not get on with the Turks. It returned to Berlin without achieving any results. Some young man went to Bagdad and Persia, but, as usual, there was more quarrelling than work even there. Some of them complained bitterly of the bigotry of the Turks. At the end a few young men remained in Berlin without any definite aims or plans.

The story of the Indians in Berlin only proves that the upper and middle classes of Indian society cannot be expected to lead the country forward. These men have a smattering of European knowledge, and the contact with European civilisation rouses their pride and ambition to a certain degree. But they have no faith or capacity. They belong to no organised Church, in India or abroad. They do not know much about their national literature and history. They are denationalised and demoralised through the influence of their unnatural environment. Their whole life is a hothouse growth. Nothing great or noble can come from this effete class, wherever its representatives may try to work. They will always be indolent, vain, egotistic and incompetent. Their character has no deep roots in religious principles or national institutions. Religion and nationality are the two great forces that mould human character. A healthy and normal society is organised as a Church and a State. The upper and middle classes of India do not belong to any Church or State. They have lost faith in the old Indian creeds, and have found no new evangel. They have lost their national independence, but they have not yet learned to love and cherish the institution known as the British Empire. Their souls must therefore languish and wither in a spirtitual vacuum. I cannot suggest any infallible remedies for this distemper; but I have here supplied a sound diagnosis. Time will show if the malady is curable. Of course, these remarks do not apply to the people living in the semi-independent Indian States.

The experience of the Indian Nationalists in Berlin confirms my opinion that the Germans are an anti-social and unreliable people, especially the Prussians, who occupy the position of leadership. After four years of unremitting activity for the German cause, one of them wrote : "The German treat even their best friends as mere agents." Another prominent member of the association said : "You may give your life for them, but they never trust you." On another occasion he remarked : "I am sorry I came to Berlin" (from the United States). "I have lost my last chance of returning to India. A young Indian gentleman served the German Government so faithfully in the Near East that he was awarded the Iron Cross. But our hero had the unpleasant experience of being put in prison some time after his return to Berlin, probably because he had criticised some German officials or quarrelled with one of the "bosses" of the association. I do not know all the facts of the case, but such amenities of the Indo-Germanic life in Berlin gave the Indians a bad name in Oriental society. It may be affirmed that all the Indians are thoroughly disgusted with the Germans, but they cannot say so. India should know that the few Indian who have worked with the Germans during the war have not the slightest desire to repeat the experiment. We have learned much, and we do not wish to have anything to do with the Germans again.

I may be excused for adding an autobiographical note at this point. I spent about forty-four months in Germany and Turkey, from February, 1915, to October, 1918. I went from Switzerland to Berlin in the last week of January, 1915, and worked earnestly till February, 1916, with the Germans and the Turks for what I then believed to be the common cause of

India and Germany. During that one year I learned that the triumph of Germany would be a great calamity for Asia and the whole world. On account of differences of opinion I made up my mind to return to Switzerland. During the winter of 1915-16 I twice asked the responsible German official for a passport for the journey to Switzerland, politely adding that I wished to return to Switzerland for the benefit of my health. Of course, he know why I had decided to steave Germany. At first he said that he advised me as a friend to stay in Germany. But he threw off the mask the second time, and replied in these words : "You will on no account be allowed to leave Germany." I then knew how matters stood. I found myself in a very dangereous position, as I was evidently regarded as an "anti-German" Oriental. In the summer of 1916 even my local correspondence was intercepted by the Berlin police. I was, of course, very anxious about the future, as these German bureaucrats might treat me as an enemy, and I was completely in their power. During three years, from February, 1916, to February, 1919, I was compelled to resort to falsehood and dissimulation in self-defence, and I look back upon that time as a period of utter degradation. But I was not a free agent. At last I persuaded the German officials that my persecution was really due to a misunderstanding, and obtained permission in November, 1917, to go to Stock-holm for propaganda. For a long time I could not get the Swedish "visa" for the journey. Circumstances beyond my control also prevented me from writing, speaking, or working openly according to my real convictions during four months after my arrival in Stockholm on October 10th, 1918. At last I was happy to be able to sever all connection with the German Government on February 20th, 1919, when I voluntarily returned my German passport to the German Legation in Stockholm. As I was detained in Germany during nearly one and a half years, and could not go to a neutral country, my health suffered very much on account of the scarcity of food in Germany. All the other Orientals and Indians went to neutral countries from time to time for short holiday; and the German official himself ran to Switzerland to eat and drink. But I was not allowed to go, as I was under the official ban from February, 1916, to

November, 1917. The German Government inflicted all this loss of time and health on me by keeping me against my will in Germany after the winter of 1915-16. This incident also illustrates German autocratic and bureaucratic methods. I insert these personal details only because I believe that my Indian friends may be interested in them.

I think I may here mention my visit to Sir Roger Casement in Berlin. He was staying at the Hotel Continental. I was introduced with other friends, by a common acquaintance. Sir Roger was very affable and made a favourable impression on all who saw him . This was in 1916, in the early period of the war. I had no discussion with him, as the disparity of age was a bar to familiarity. But I can assert without fear of contradiction that Sir Roger Casement was deeply disappointed at the close of his stay in German. At first his friends commented on his habit of spending much time in Munich instead of Berlin, where political questions were supposed to be settled. He had come on a political mission, and was expected to be in close touch with the highest authorities of the realm. But it was generally known that Sir Roger "did not like" Berlin. This strange "dislike" of the capital of the Empire, whose support he solicited for his Fatherland, appeared to me to betoken want of tact. But how could an experienced man like him be wanting in tact ? I was rather puzzled till I heard some one say : "They did not treat him well here in Berlin." Thus I learned that it was the some old story of arrogance and rudeness. Truly, the Prussians are no respecters of persons in these matters ! Finally, a German friend of Sir Roger's said to me : "He had no high opinion of the Germans. He used to say 'They don't know their own mind. They make promises which they do not keep. They are dishonourable.' He was very much disappointed." When I listened to these words I confirmed in my own views on the question. Sir Roger casement, the elderly gentleman and much-travelled diplomat, who had seen the world and known much more about it than a studious youth like myself, has expressed this opinion as his verdict against Germany. The Orientals may distrust my judgment, but they cannot surely dismiss Sir Roger's severe indictment with contempt. Sir Roger Casement must be heard, and his testimony is given against these Germans.

The German adventure in Asia has ended in complete disaster. Friends of freedom can now survey the world with less dismay than in the winter of 1917-18. The Germans got their chance through the unaccountable folly of the Turks. Germany conquered Turkey without a blow, for the Turks themselves opened the doors for these greedly birds of prey. Personal influence played an important part in Turkey, and two or three men were really responsible for this rash step. The Turks were also too much in a hurry. They declared war on the Entente only three months after the outbreak of hostilities in Europe. They could not judge who would win the war. It was the puerile short-sightedness and impetousity of hot- headed youths. The older men advised a policy of waiting and watching. Turkey knew that she had some moral influence in the Islamic world; and that England and France had millions of Muhammadan subjects. But she deliberately allied herself with the German Imperialists, and deserves no sympathy now. History cannot undo what has been done. As Lowell says :

"Once to every man and nation comes the moment to decide,
In the strife of Truth with Falsehood, 'twixt the good and evil side :
Some great Cause, God's new Messiah, offering each the bloom or blight,
Parts the goats upon the left hand and the sheep upon the right,
And the choice goes by for ever 'twixt that Darkness and that Light."

The Turks allowed the Germans to enter Asia in their thousands. But the result has been just the reverse of what was expected. The Germans have failed miserably, not only from the military standpoint, but also in a moral sense. They are now hated and despised wherever they have shown themselves during the war, from Stamboul to Kabul, and from Medina to

Teheran. This is the outcome of four years of German intrigue and diplomacy in Asia. Whatever may happen in future, no German is likely to inspire confidence in the East, and Germany will never be able to carry out any programme of Oriental politics. Germany is to-day morally bankrupt in Asia.

The causes of this interesting phenomenon are various and manifold. The Germans soon showed that they were no friends of Turkey and Persia. They were discovered to be wolves in sheep's clothing. They professed to come as allies and champions of the Orient, but they could not even conceal their selfish designs in the Near East. They convinced all Orientals that their real objects were plunder and conquest. They did not sincerely wish that Turkey and Persia should be helped to free themselves from the incubus of European imperialism for ever. They only wanted that the Germans should rule and exploit the Asiatics instead of the Russians. It was the old story of the horse, the stag, and the man over again. Falsehood and hypocrisy in this essential matter alienated all who were at first disposed to welcome them in spite of their faults. German ambition was so impatient that it could not even adopt the language of courtesy and amity.

The Germans, by their words and deeds, repelled every Oriental patriot, and caused a revulsion of feeling in favour of England. During the war the Germans have been the worst enemies of Germany everywhere. A German officer, who was travelling with an Egyptian Nationalist leader, said in course of conversation: "Would you prefer a German occupation of Egypt?" This characteristic remark was, of course, repeated and passed from mouth to mouth. I took a trip on the Bosphorus with a young German official, and we talked of the future of Turkey. I said: "What Turkey has a better Government and more money the Bosphorus will grow into a much-frequented summer resort. It is more beautiful than the Riviera in winter." To my surprise, the German replied: "Yes, but the Turks can't do anything. We should rule here." I didn't know what to say to this indiscreet imperialist after such a cynical confession. I can cite only such incidents as came under my personal observation. I guess that the official courier of the German Embassy must have transmitted interesting correspondence with regard to the aggressive plans of German statesmen in Asia. Those documents must be in the German archives, and may be given to the world some day. I can speak only as a private person, whose sources of information were limited to occasional conversation with friends and acquaintances. A Turkish official said to me : "The Germans have refused to build a modern arsenal for us here, as they do not wish to make us strong. Their idea is that they may rule over us in future if we remain weak." Such was the much-trumpeted friendship of the Germans for the Turks! I am sure that the Germans must have divulged their real intentions in a thousand different ways, as they worked with the Turks and the Persians at that time. The German press did not take care to be reticent or hypocritical. The newspapers wrote in tones of exultation about German expansion in Mesopotamia and the bright prospects in Persia. All this incriminating testimony convinced the Turks and the Persians that they had to deal with very dangerous enemies.

The Germans could not get on with the Turks, the Arabs and the Persians, especially as the majority of them were Prussians. The incurable boorishness and tactlessness of the Prussians made co-operation impossible. A Hungarian officer related to me how some German officers threw Turkish gentlemen out of a railway carriage in order to get seats for themselves. Such incidents must have occurred very frequently, as it was the general opinion that the Germans had no manners. This fault is enough to ruin a man in Asia, for we Orientals believe that courtesy is the beginning of morality, and I think we are right. A man who cannot even be polite must certainly be an unsociable creature. The Prussians failed at Bagdad on account of their inability to work with the Turks there. There was nothing but continual friction and personal bickering all the time.

"The churl in spirit, howe'er he veil
His want in forms for fashion's sake,
Will let his coltish nature break
At seasons through the gilded pale."

With the Germans, however, the "coltish nature" was very much on the surface. Such people may be in their element at Potsdam, but they are utterly unfit for political enterprises in Asia. The German cannot divest himself of his character simply by crossing the Hellespont; for who can escape from himself ? A Muslim scholar, who travelled with a German mission to a distant country, at last wrote that the "ill-tempered" Prussian officer, who has his colleague, had marred all chances of success at the court of the Asiatic ruler. Another Oriental gentleman, who also took part in this mission, was so deeply offended with the Prussian officer that he ceased to be on speaking terms with him after a short time, and subsequently drew up an indictment consisting of more than sixty articles against him! He also wrote from Bagdad, which was only the first stage on the journey : "I cannot bear slights all the time." This Prussian hero did not know how to behave towards others; he was so full of self-importance and German conceit that he lost all sense of proportion. The Prussians are experts in the art of losing friends. They have great projects of world dominion, but they don't know that diplomacy without manners cannot succeed.

The Germans have not only behaved like uncultivated barbarians in personal intercourse in Asia, but they have also acted like false and unprincipled scoundrels. This is a much more serious matter, which touches the very kernel of the question. The Germans do not keep faith with their colleagues; they are untruthful and untrustworthy. Their word cannot be trusted. In spite of their much-advertised "Kultur," they have not learned the simple virtue of of truthfulness. They also do not know that "honesty is the best policy" in the long run. They set out on a campaign of world-empire and pitted their strength against the English. But they did not provide themselves with the armour that the Englishman wears in the East.

The English are on the whole a truthful people; that is perhaps their characteristic virtue. Whatever policy the State may adopt, the individual Englishman is a reliable person. He keeps his word. And the English Government also keeps faith with its friends, partly from policy, and partly from the national habit of truthfulness. The Englishman has acquired a reputation for truthfulness in Asia. Several years ago a hotel proprietor in a small island in the West Indies said to me : "The English are different from other people. If an Englishman says he will do a thing, you may be sure that he will do it." The Englishman also trusts others, as he wishes that he should be trusted. An Egyptian Nationalist, who is a violent anti-British agitator, said to me : "If a man works with the English they will never believe anything against him." This virtue of truthfulness gains friends and makes co-operation possible.

But with the Germans it is all the other way. They wish only to exploit their Oriental colleagues and then to desert or ill-treat them. They make promises and never keep them, as Sir Roger Casement also found out too late. A Government must never cheat its friends, or it will soon have no friends at all. And a diplomat's word must be as good as his bond. The Germans have acted like a dishonest, short-sighted business man. But they could not help it; they could not change their national character in a day. A German promised a reward of £60 to a poor Indian who had saved his life in Arabia; he gave the promise in writing.

But the Germans in Constantinople thought that they need not pay so much, seeing that the officer was now in safety. After much haggling they paid a small amount (perhaps £20). These are the methods of the mighty German Imperial Government in Asia! A German induced some Persian chiefs to come to Constantinople, but when they arrived there no one cared for them. They regretted very keenly that they had accepted the invitation. At last the Turks heard that they were in a difficult situation, and helped them with money and other necessaries. A German officer promised to take a young Indian with him to Persia, and told him that he should make preparations for the journey. After a few days I learned that the German had already left! The young Indian enthusiast was very angry and lost much of his ardour for the German cause.

The Englishman never plays such tricks in his dealings with individuals. I had no opportunity of travelling in Turkey and Persia during the war; but I am sure that the Germans have left behind them a damning record of broken promises, unfulfilled engagements, and unredeemed pledges all over the Near East. They will live in Oriental tradition as liars and swindlers for a long time to come, for the East does not easily forget. A Persian politician said to me: "They gave us all sorts of promises, and now we are in a worse position than before. We counted upon them, but they have done nothing." The German's unscrupulous methods have set off the Englishman's habitual truthfulness to greater advantage than ever before. The people have had the opportunity of comparing the two nations with each other. It may be affirmed that the Germans would have a much better reputation in Asia to-day if they had never gone there. In their case that fallacious proverb is certainly true: "Familiarity breeds contempt." And the reason is that they are really contemptible.

The Germans have forfeited the sympathy of the Orientals not only through their arrogance and their unreliable character, but also because they have shown themselves to be inconceivably greedy locusts. They have taken to plunder and extortion, while they pretended to come as friends and deliverers! A Turkish official said to me: "They are too greedy, and they have the wrong psychology." An Indian colleague told me that the Germans had looted banks in Persia on the pretext that they were English banks. The Persians thought that the Germans would help them to organise their country; but they found that the newcomers were bent only on carrying booty home. It is almost incredible that "honourable" German officers should even be accused of such rapacious conduct in countries where they wished to acquire prestige and influence.

But the German is capable of committing every crime in dealing with other peoples, especially as he thinks that he himself is a being of another species. He does not admit that any moral law is binding on him in his relations with foreigners, Europeans or Orientals. He pursues what he calls his "nigger-politik" towards them and treats them like primitive savages or irrational brutes. A German official expressed these sentiments in a letter, which was intercepted by the Persians by a lucky chance. The worthy Teuton was obliged to explain away his contemptuous remarks about the Orientals; but it may be imagined that he could never again be popular among the Persians. An Indian gentleman, who knows Persia well, told me that the Germans had behaved like unprincipled freebooters and blackmailers in Persia. He related several stories of their brutality and avarice in dealing with the helpless people of that unfortunate country. Well may the Orientals exclaim : "Save us from our friends."

The Germans cannot trust others, as they themselves are untrustworthy. They are always suspicious of their friends. They have very peculiar methods of work- One German is sent out to spy upon another German. I think that half the German officials or agents working in neutral countries were spying on the other half. A German journalist once said to me : "A German never trusts another German." I asked : "Is it because you know one another so well ?" He also said of the officials of a certain department : "They are all working very hard; but they are working against one another." When the Germans treat one another in this way it is easy to understand why they cannot trust foreigners. Being themselves devoid of the sense of honour, they think that others are also like them, as every man judges his neighbours by his own standard.

The entire German system of government is based on the principle of mutual spying agd backbiting. When such methods are adopted in intercourse with the Orientals the consequences are ruinous. In such co-operation the slightest rift in the lute will make the music altogether mute. I shall relate an amusing story to illustrate German methods of work. A German official received certain letters from some Persian Nationalists to forward them to other members of the party. He first opened them, thus proving that he was not a gentleman. He then gave them to another Persian journalist to translate them for him. Now it so happened that the Nationalists had warned their comrade in those letters against the wiles of this very journalist, who was regarded by them as an unscrupulous and unpatriotic charlatan. It may be imagined that the journalist was not quite pleased to read what was written about him and to see himself as the others saw him. He read the letters to the German official, perhaps omitting the passages that referred to himself. I believe he subsequestly protested to the Nationalists against the aspersions on his character.

The mean, underhand ways of the German official were thus made known to all the Orientals. We all enjoyed the joke, but also learned a lesson. Who would entrust this German again with confidential letters ? And these Germans are all alike; they all act in the same manner. We have found it out in the course of prolonged experience of their habits. They can never gain the esteem or good-will of Oriental gentlemen. An Oriental gentleman, who joined a German mission to an Asiatic Court, was placed in a very undignified position on his arrival in that distant land, as the German officer did not supply him with money, and he was finally treated as a guest by his new friends. He had come as one of the diplomatic representatives of the German Empire, but had to stay as a beggar. He had sacrificed much for the Germans, but he did not receive a single farthing for his work from the German officer. I am sure he would never have come to Berlin if he had known the Germans before.

But we were all ignorant of German aims, methods and moral standards, as the Germans had never come into close contact with the Orientals before the war. German ingratitude and baseness can go so far that the Prussian officer even tried to get him locked up as a lunatic on his return to Berlin in the spring of 1918, after a journey full of great hardships and perils! And a responsible German official conveyed to him the comforting message that he would not be allowed to leave the countries of Germany's allies. Thus he was practically interned by the Germans, after he had made such enormous sacrifices for what we in 1915 erroneously believed to be the common cause of India and Germany! Such is ths guerdon of all who work for or with the Germans. It is necessary that all India should know this sequel of the story.

The German autocrats must not fancy that they can exploit and persecute honest Orientals with impunity. There is nothing hidden that shall not be made public, so long as I have the power to speak and write. I have heard from an Indian Nationalist that the Germans are also responsible for the prosecution of the Indian Nationalists in the United States, as the German officials gave over to the American police the cypher with which documentary evidence against our misguided and impulsive young patriots could be obtained. In plain words, the Germans betrayed their Indian colleagues! The American Government must be praised for the leniency with which our countrymen have been treated by the liberal-minded judges of that great Republic, for they had put themselves in a very dangerous predicament by intriguing with the Germans. The Americans knew that the Germans were characterless adventurers, but the Indians did not. If my information is correct no words can measure the depths of infamy to which the Germans can sink. They must be shunned as utterly unsociable and immoral bipeds. It is to be hoped that these young Indian enthusiasts will also give up the fruitless revolutionary methods which have made them the dupes of cunning German imperialists during this war.

The Orient has learned that it made a bad bargain when it accepted the German alliance. A leading Turkish newspaper recently wrote: "We do not like the Germans. And the

Germans themselves are to blame for this." These words sum up the judgment of the Turks on their allies. The Germans have had a great chance, but they have lost it, because they are morally unfit for such great tasks. This is the lesson of the four years' work in common. The German inroad into Asia will remain in the memory of Oriental nations as a troubled dream. Now they must be awaked to the sober reality, which teaches them that their destiny is linked with that of the English people for a very long time to come.

Every tale must have a moral. And may garrulous war notes are also intended to emphasise certain truths which have been brought home to us during the war. No thinking man can remain the same after this war as he was before it. A Lowell says, "New occasions teach new duties."

We must now learn that England has a moral and historical mission in Asia. The English people have built up an empire in Asia and Africa during the last two hundred years. They had previously prepared themselves for this task by establishing free institutions at home and developing a great and noble literature. This empire has its roots deep in the historical forces and movements of the past. It is not a mushroom growth. It is not based on the quicksands of mere ambition and exploitation. It has shown itself to be a solid structure founded on the rock of historical necessity and British wisdom.

The Germans counted upon a revolt in Ireland and South Africa, a general insurrection of all the Muslims, and a rebellion in India. They also hoped that some Allies would desert the Entente. None of these hopes have been fulfilled. Irish "Nationalism," the great Jihad, and Indian and Egyptian "extremism" have been found to be puny forces compared with British imperialism. England has also managed to keep her Allies together in spite of the reverses and vicissitudes of the military struggle during four years. A nation's character and wisdom are put to the test in such crises. Germany has been weighed in the balance and found wanting. Great Britain has vindicated her title to her vast empire. The English colonies have loyally responded to the call of the Mother Country; the

Asiatic colonies have rendered assistance, or created no difficulties at such a perilous time.

The Boers have stood faithfully by England. A nation that can save such an empire in the face of various and enormous difficulties must be recognised as the trustee of the future of Asia and Africa. British character and British statesmanship will preserve this heritage for a long time, and the storms of jealousy and intrigue will beat against it in vain. The British Empire is an institution that has come to stay. In this respect it resembles the ancient Roman Empire and the Spanish Empire in America. We can have our different plans and programmes for the development of this empire; but the institution will remain a single political unit during several centuries. It will of course undergo a process of evolution in the right direction, for progress is the law of life for all organisations. The stability of the British Empire is a salient fact that emerges from the dust and smoke of the war.

We have also learned that the dissolution of the British and the French Empires in Asia and Africa would result only in a change of masters for the people of those regions. The Germans wished to acquire the French colonies and the territory of the Ottoman Empire. The world is a battlefield for the powerful imperialists of all nations; and the weak and disorganised Oriental nations are only the pawns in the game. They cannot establish or maintain free national States in this era of armed imperialism. They must live and die as friends and proteges of the great Powers. Under these circumstances, English and French imperialism is a thousand times preferable to German or Japanese imperialism. The English and the French have free institutions at home; and they are morally the most advanced of all the great nations of the world.

The people of Asia and Africa must make common cause with these two nations, and try to assimilate their culture and ideals. In course of time they will be admitted as equal citizens of these States. Intrigue with the enemies of England and France will lead only to disaster. If the other nations, which may set up as rivals of England and France, succeed in their aims, they will rule over us, and our last state will be worse than the first. If they fail they will betray us, and we shall suffer. In either case, the will-o'-the-wisp of intransigent "nationalism" and race-hatred would land us in the bogs of misery and misfortune. The Ukrainians intrigued with the Germans in order to "free" themselves from Russian "tyranny"; but they found that the Germans were worse masters than the Russians. They repented bitterly of their folly when they began to perceive the ruinous effects of their policy.

The Turks refused to come to terms with England and France, and to-day they curse the Germans. Experience teaches us that the feeble peoples should work with the great nations which have already organised the vast empires in Asia and Africa. Disruption can only expose them to much greater evils than those from which they suffer under the present system. Co-operation and evolution should be our watch-words. The policy of separation and intrigue is futile and fallacious.

The Muslims of India and Egypt should lay aside their religious bigotry and work with the English and the French for the acquisition of modern citizenship. Religion is a private affair in the modern world. The Jihad has been found to be a vain cry. The mountain of Islamic fanaticism has brought forth the little mouse of local riots and tumults. The Caliphate is in liquidation. The Muslims should learn that London and Paris are the centres of world-politics to-day. They should give up the dreams of Pan-Islamism, and set to work as loyal British and French citizens to raise themselves to the level of European civilisation. They should let the dead past bury its dead, and prepare themselves for the glorious tasks that await them in the States to which they now belong.

East and West must unite for the realisation of these new ideals. The English and the French must get rid of race-prejudice and pride. The Orientals must lay aside distrust and rancour. The two languages in which the message of freedom was first delivered to the modern world should be studied and loved in Asia and Africa. English and French will serve to unite the Orient and the Occident in indissoluble bonds of comradeship. For us, Indians and Egyptians, English literature should be a treasure of untold worth. English history should be a mine of the noblest wisdom for us and our children. England has much to give us besides protection and organisation. We are now heirs to all that the Englishman holds in fee as his birthright. England is free and great, and we can share in this freedom and greatness as worthy citizens of the greatest State that the world has yet seen. England will achieve what Alexander dreamed of and what Rome partially accomplished. We, too, are called to this work. If we help to realise this ideal, generations yet unborn will bless our names. The future keeps its secret, but we must do our duty in this spirit, looking forward to the advent of the time—

"When the war-drum throbs no longer, and the battle-flag is furled.

In the Parliament of Man, the Federation of the World."

4

The Assessment

Har Dayal, a agreat patriot, played a significant role during the freedom movement of our sub-continent. In his early days he was greatly impressed by the political philosophy of Tilak, Lajpat Rai, Aurobindo Ghose Khudiram and other prominent Indians who were engaged in the freedom struggle. He suffered much but did not give up his political ideology which was anti-colonial rule in contents. Time and again, he urged the people of India to develop a united stand against the Raj if they wanted independence.

Har Dayal talked about the social upliftment of women in our society. He was of the view that they should not remain backward in any sense. He devised ways and means for their economic development. "The life of the middle and upper classes is artificial in the extreme. Women attach too much importance to the conservation of their beauty and youth. They also fear a very large family. Constant excitement also renders them unfit for motherhood. The result is the wide prevalence of nervous disorders among women, and an increasing degree of artificial sterility. Marriage is regarded more a means of gratification than as an institution for multiplying and replenishing the earth. Surely there must be something rotten in the social system which is thus running to suicide. Over-population is not desirable, but the degeneracy of women as a physical type is a very serious evil. There is something wrong somewhere either in the ethical or the economic conditions of such a society, for natural instincts can never be warped and perverted except under the influence of radically vicious surroundings. Man can defeat nature, but he must become terribly wicked and foolish or miserably unfortunate before he can succeed. Thus an individual commits suicide, when he is insane or frightfully wretched. A similar rule applies to social phenomena of the kind that we have been considering."

He has something to say about the working-classes too : "The nation does not live in the palace or the cottage, but in the slums. If you wish to find the real West, go to the slums. The working classes constitute the nation. And the position of woman among them is one of such terrible hardship and misery that no one who has seen them, can bear the sickening cant of Christian missionaries and others about the 'higher position' of woman in Europe without uttering that appropriate injunction first employed for protection against shameless and extravagent mendacity in Grimm's fairy tales : 'Open the window that these lies may escape.'

"Women and men sleep like beasts in these hovels and poverty often obliges them to take strangers as lodgers even in that one room ! This is civilized Europe that brings together such hosts and such paying guests ! The women are pale and haggard, with sunken eyes and hollow cheeks. Premature death is their only friend. The horrors of negro-slavery are only read in books, but the worse horrors of wage-slavery are there for all to see today in every town of the West, under all flags and skies. No Turkish woman or Soudanese slave leads such a life of unremitting toil and brutish squalor. This is an almost nadir of human degradation and it is found in the West, which is said to honour women. This is civilized Europe which kills out the maternal instinct by luxury among the rich, and want among the poor ! This stage marks the last gasp of the women's depair. Woman has been reduced to a condition of wretchedness, compared with which the harem and the kraal are heaven itself. Congresses meet to discuss the 'white slave traffic', which is an organised trade now as it was in the days of Haroon-al-Rashid or the Mahdi. Modern Europe is not a whit better in this respect than Morocco or old Turkestan. The 'maiden tribute is exacted by the rich and the profligate from the working classes today as it was in antiquity. Thus Europe honours its women !"

The women of India, says he in Optimism, are eminently fitted to play a prominent part in the coming change. They are loyal to persons, and this is the next best virtue after loyalty to principles. They are conservative in many respects, and healthy conservatism is today a sign of individuality among less-advanced communities attacked by the aggressive semi-civilization of Europe. Hindu women are also very simple in their habits. They will not work spontaneously for the public good, because they are not very intelligent, but they will work through the influence of personality. Every young man should be a missionary public spirit to his wife, and he will have a very willing convert. "The young husbands of India have an enormous responsibility to discharge towards their wives in this respect."

"The fundamental rule of social duty is this : Let all your thoughts and actions promote the development and happiness of all mankind. The family is your smallest sphere of activity in the service of Humanity. It is composed of yourself, your wife, and children. This group is a natural biological unit. Man and woman are attracted to each other by sex-passion and personal love, and the pledge of their lives is the offspring. Like all good things, it may be used wisely, or it may be abused. At present alas ! man and woman are guilty of wicked, shameless, and criminal abuse of this natural and necessary institution. They suffer from the psychological malady that Gastano Mosca has called 'familyism'. Family-egotism prompts many people to rob their neighbours and ruin the State. It makes honest public life impossible, as every politician tries to benefit his family at the expense of the State. This moral failing accounts for the very slow growth of public spirit in such countries as China, Persia, and India. In contemporary society, marriage and domestic life have robbed many progressive movements of some of their most zealous propagandists. Before marriage many men and women work for different causes and ideals with exemplary enthusiasm; but they are apt to neglect this higher duty when they have a family to love and care for. Marriage has ruined many a noble character ! Many brave men are afraid of imprisonment and loss of money, simply because they are blessed with a wife and children. Marriage makes cowards of them all. Surely there is some truth in Bacon's shrewd remark : 'He that hath wife and children hath given hostages to fortune; for they are impediments to great enterprises, either of virtue or mischief.' Or shall we say with the cynic : 'A young man married is a man that's marred'?"

"Shall we then cry", Har Dayal questions, "Down with the family'?" But before discussing this extreme he considers two points : "The relation of lovers (as a loving couple) is natural and beneficial. It may be bio-psychological, or purely psychological. I believe that men and women have a natural tendency to form couples according to the law of affinity. We must accept Nature's law of couple building as we accept sex and love. Two lovers must have a certain special relation to each other, which is expressed in complete confidence, deep joy in each other's company and mutual service. Love is a specialized form of friendship between man and a woman, whom it unites as a couple.

"Just as we do not demand the annihilation of the individual as a safeguard against personal egotism, even so it is not necessary to abolish the couple-relation in order to counteract the disastrous effects of familyism. We teach each individual to serve the great human Society; and we should teach each couple to do the same. No natural group should be whittled away or condemned : it should only be subordinated to the highest universal group, which is Humanity. Beware of the vice of couple-egotism; do not make plans only for your own success and happiness. Do not worry too much about money. Do not neglect old friends, who were dear to you before love shone on your path. Remember that he is after all not the most important man that lives, and that she is not the most wonderful woman in the world. Do not idolize and idealize each other too much. If your love makes you more selfish and avaricious than before, then it is a curse, and not a blessing. True love should always develop human personality, and never dwarf it. This is its proper function. It should inspire been man and woman to make the best use of their bodies and minds and to consecrate them to the progress of Society." Har Dayal wanted to harness both the black horse, the body and the white horse, the soul, and he wanted them to run in neatly parallel lines for the sake of the individual and society.

"Love makes your ascent to the Ideal easier, if you remain its master; but it can also hurl you quickly to perdition, if you become its slave. Higher than love, beyond mere personal joy, sits conscience enthroned in eternal majesty. Conscience is the Guide, and love must follow it. Love is not an end in itself : it is a means to a social end. Perfect harmony in conjugal life should be aimed at. But harmony must be striven for : it will not come by itself. Respect each other's individuality : do not try to impose your will on your partner. Never forget Lessing's precept : 'Equality is always the strongest tie of love.' Be ready to accept each other's plans and suggestions, unless you discern some grave danger in them. Yield to each other in everyday matters : most couples quarrel over trivial affairs. Disarm petulance with a sweet smile, and answer small complaints with friendly silence. Do not attempt always to have the last word. Divine unspoken wishes with the wisdom of true love, and fulfil them as the opportunity presents itself. Love starts the married life, but unselfishness sustains and prolongs it. The happiness of a couple depends on character, not on violent emotion and passion."

"We believe that women should own property, receive a liberal education, and devote their genius or talent to art, science and literature. They should be able to follow a trade or profession, vote at the elections, and be eligible for election to public assemblies. All useful offices of the State should be open to them. They should be allowed to teach and preach in colleges and churches according to their capacity. They should give themselves in marriage without promising to 'obey' the man. They should take part in amateur sport and athletics. They should receive equal and adequate remuneration for all work done anywhere. . . .in the home, the factory, the office, the studio, the laboratory, the hospital and the gymnasium. They should not be debarred from any form of useful activity on account of sex. Personality is sacred, and it is not masculine or feminine, but simply human. Genious and talent are scattered broadcast by Nature without any sex-prejudice. Nature is not niggardly towards woman, far from it. The male has deprived woman, of freedom and equality, and thereby also robbed himself of her services and contributions to Progress. Many potential female statesmen have sewed buttons on trousers, and not a few of Nature's gifted scientists have experimented only with soups and puddings. How much precious brain-matter has been lost in the kitchen and harem ! What a loss to Humanity through centuries of history ! What folly and pride in the Male masquerading as a demigod ! How many women have lived and died in dumb obscurity, who could have been like Apasia, Zenobia, Sappho, Hypatia, Rabia, Gargi, Ahalya Bai, Naidu, Blavatsky, Browning, Stowe, Besant, Ramabai, Siddons, Lind, and many others.

"Humanism condemns all laws, customs and institutions that hinder women from developing her personality to the highest perfection. We humanists neither exalt nor decry womanhood; we do not deal in superlatives either way. We treat women as we treat men." "Both men and women are and will be virtuous and wicked, clever and stupid, wise and foolish, lovable or detestable. We do not adore woman, and we do not despise her. Woman is neither an angel nor a devil : she is simply a human being, we take a common-sense view of this question."

"Freedom for woman should not mean freedom to make a fool of herself." Equality with man should not be interpreted as equality in vice and self-indulgence. If this precept is disregarded, then women will not be able to do much good to themselves or the man in the new era of emancipation. Freedom cuts both ways. It can lift you up the zenith of developed human personality or drag you down to the nadir of mere sub-human sentiency. Equality also is a two-edged sword : it can be understood as equality in virtue and knowledge, or as equality in frivolity and degeneracy. The emancipated African slave may acquire education and is free to rise, so is he free to fall, for all artificial props and restraints have been removed. He has left protected servitude behind, with all its advantages, and disadvantages. So has also woman.

The modern woman is free. She should add new virtues to the old virtues of the domestic guarded woman. She should not learn new vices from Man, while she also loses the old-fashioned virtues. Such a result would be a sad social tragedy. Woman has always shrunk instinctively from the narcotics and stimulants, in which foolish Man has indulged so freely at all epochs. This old feminine distaste for alcohol and tobacoo has been justified by modern hygiene and eugenics. Now the modern woman should wean us Men from our bad habits, and not join us in our barbarous alcoholism and nicotinism. Liquor, tobacco and other drugs did not poison the blood of the mothers of the race in the old society but now many 'modern' Women rejoice in the frothy and reeking equality of the tankard and the cigar. Such equality cannot be a blessing. The modern woman should be Man's mentor and monitor, not his frivolous boorcompanion and fellow-roysterer.

Perhaps the most important thing is that the modern woman should guard the sexual purity of the old-fashioned wife, while she acquires manifold new graces and accomplishments. In Man and Woman, Sex is of the soul first and foremost. Dogs and pigs do not fall in love or write Petrarchian sonnets, but men and women do. As we leave the primevalslime behind,

Sex becomes more of a soul-impulse and less of a physical appetite. Humanism teaches that Sex is not the contact of two bodily organs, but the mutual acceptance of two personalities for personal growth, and racial development. Without the deepest love and the highest social ideal, Sex is a mere stud-and-farm phenomenon, Iago's 'master and man exercise.' But Sex among civilized men and women is the poetry of life, the perfume of the Rose of Dante's Beatific Vision. The modern woman must teach and train Men to love purity and chastity: she should not sink to the level of the sensual primitive Male. She can now prove that her chastity is of choice, and not chance, as it could frequently be under the old regime. She can now demonstrate that she is not the slave of the Sex, but its mistress and priestess. She must understand that Sex in Man and Woman is not a mere physiological function, but in very truth a mirror of the soul. If the mirror is dimmed or cracked, the light of the soul will also cease to shine bright and clear. There is a mysterious and inexplicable connexion between Sex and the imponderable tone and texture of the whole Personality. You cannot analyse it, but you can feel and sense it. Without purity and chastity, Man or Woman is like a faded flower, a lack-lustre gem, or a puddle of muddy water. Woman may then be valued as a sexual tool by a few coarse and clever hedonists. But she will not command the respect and esteem of the typical modern Humanist, who has been admitted into holiest arcana of love and idealism. "The more the modern woman learns to say Noli me tangers ('touch me not') the greater will be the cultural gifts bestowed on all of us through her new freedom and equality. Woman can raise us to higher heights or fall with us to lower depths. Which shall it be?"

Married persons can call to their aid the examples of those 'notable couples who have helped each other in the pursuit of noble aims and ideas'. I have given one example. Here is another : Crates and Hipparchia were philosopher-comrades in an age when most women received no higher education. "She fell in love with the discourse and the life of Crates, writes Laertius, and would not pay attention to any of her suitors, their wealth, their high birth, or their beauty. But to her Crates was everything. She used even to threaten her parents that she would kill herself unless she were given in marriage to him. Crates, therefore, was implored by her parents to dissuade the girl, and he did all he could. At last, failing to persuade her, he got up, took his clothes before her face, and said, "This is the bridegroom : here is his property : make your choice accordingly, for you will be no helpmate of mine unless you share my pursuits." The girl chose; and, adopting the same dress, went about her husband, and lived with him in public.

In modern times, many couples have grown together in service and achievement. One such, Bhai Balmukand and Ram Rakkhi, to whom I have referred earlier, will shine in the firmament for all times to come.

Nobody can ignore another facet of married life : "love makes couples, and couples beget children. Parenthood has a psychological as well as a physiological basis. Love without children is bare and bleak indeed. Parenthood opens for us a new world of deep emotions and creative impulses. It is the crowning glory of the long travail of Evolution. Parental love, which is based on physiology, may become a blind, raging, tearing passion. If it is related directly to the purely psychological need, it will probably be exhibited as a sweet and gentle emotion, which will produce no antic-social effects at all."

Family, therefore, should be subordinated to Society in the true social spirit. "Gautama Buddha left his family in order to enter on his spiritual quest; and he later persuaded his wife and son to accept poverty and dedicate themselves to the service of Humanity." (Har Dayal, too, cut himself off from his family and took to the life of a friar.) In certain cases 'men and women could overcome family-egotism in the service of the larger comunity.' A very beautiful example of such idealism was provided by St. Perpetua. She was twenty-two, well educated and married. Her parents were living. She had two brothers, and a son, a babe at the breast. She was arrested, but she refused to recant, and was condemned to death. She was first tossed by an infuriated cow, and then killed. An ancient document describes her super-human psychology in her own words : "While we were still with the persecutors, my father persisted in seeking to turn me away and cast me down from the faith. After a few days, we were taken into the dungeon. I obtained leave for my infant to remain in the dungeon with me and suckled him. Another day we were suddenly taken away to be heard and arrived at the town-hall. In my anxiety for the child, I addressed my mother and comforted my brother, and commended my son their to care. We mounted the platform. The procurator said, 'Spare the grey hairs of your father, spare the infancy of your boy. Offer sacrifice for the well-being of the Emperors.' I replied, 'I will not do so.' "

"How would you explain the sexual life of Har Dayal ?"— These words were addressed to me by a learned scholar. He explained himself : "For an intelligent worker it is perhaps very necessary that he should have a companion : he cannot do without one." Most probably he himself had some difficulty in this respect and hence this question.

Har Dayal, too, while at Oxford, read Herbert Spencer. But he needed no Herbert Spencer to goad him to work as a patriot. Still he had respect for him at these words show : "We need many saintly scholars and scholarly saints, like Confucius, Plato, Hemachandra, Al-Farabi, Aristotle, Zeno, Albertus Magnus, Roger Bacon, Herbert Spencer and others." Again, Jack London, through his novel The little Lady of the Big House, has tried to convey that Har Dayal was building up the philosophy which Herbert Spencer and August Comte had elaborated. "He's a revolutionalist of sorts. He's dabbled in our universities, studied in France, Italy, Switzerland; is a political refugee from India, and he's hitched his wagon to two stars : one, a new synthetic system of philosophy : the other, rebellion against the tyranny of British rule in India. He advocates individual terrorism and direct mass action." Har

Dayal has discussed Comte's Positivism in his Twelve Religions.

"We must all realize that patriotism is the root of all national progress and freedom," thus wrote Lala Har Dayal when he was 54, a few days before his death in 1939. Thirty years earlier, when he was hardly twenty-five, Mr. Gokhale, who admired him, had a talk for several hours at the end of which he remarked : "Har Dayal is mad after the country !" Nationalism was his ruling passion and had been since the time he was a student at Oxford. In 1907 he believed in "the establishment of Swarajya in India through the progressive application of the principle of Dissociation from the British administration."

During this period he drew up "A Sketch of a Complete Movement for the Emancipation of India," and the Society of Political Missionaries was founded. This was the object of his affection. The aim of the society was "Actual preparation for the inevitable struggle, whether diplomatic, military or other." The technique was simple : "Complete self-dedication." It was not a secret organization but a quiet movement. He stated : "We must work quietly till we are a strong and well-organized party which can withstand any amount of opposition."

On account of Lala Har Dayal's attitude towards the throwing of the bomb on the Viceroy at Delhi the Indian students in San Francisco were nervously agitated and excited. (On the other hand it had altogether different effect on Har Dayal : "The Delhi Bomb is on of the sweetest and loveliest bombs.") When he was questioned about this he was very frank and gave out his mind : "He saw the need of supporting the Indian War of Independence in every possible way. Now that it had begun in the City of Delhi, it must be carried everywhere."

Har Dayal gave his suggestions with regard to improving the political status of India. "Oh, it is a big thing," replied he. "The ambition is quite good and laudable. But the first thing is this : How are we going to be free ? I hold that we should found public schools on the lines of those in Eton and Harrow and produce statesmen and builders of the nation. They should, I think, be able to guide the people on right lines in all the departments of life." But where ? "In Nepal." Why in Nepal ? "Nepal is free from the slavery of the British. She is free from Western influence, too. Again, the Nepalese have new blood, new life in them. Besides, they are a simple people. The geographical position of Nepal is also very good, perhaps unique. They are well-protected; natural forces are defending them. Once I decided to go to Nepal. While staying in Sweden I drew up a plan about this. I thought of crossing Russia into Tibet and from there going to Nepal. But the scheme was rather odd because it would have taken me good time and the expenses, too, would have been considerable. Later on this idea cropped up : I should go to India first and, not staying there, proceed to Nepal."

In his Hints for Self-Culture he has opposed the idea of a nation-state. "The nation-state may be truly compared to the dinosaurs and the tryannosaun's of the Mesozoic Age. Like those gigantic reptiles, the sovereign nation-state has a very small brain with which to think and plan, but tremendously powerful teeth and claws to tear and rend, to destroy and dismember." The nation-state is in "all devouring monster," because "every institution in every country is at present slowly but surely assimilated to Nationalism, as all plants and animals are petrified in the rock."

"If history is studied in a scientific and cosmopolitan spirit, a new era must be employed for reckoning dates and periods of time. There have been several national eras, e.g., the Hellenic system of the Olympiads, the Roman era which began with the year of the foundation of Rome, the Vikrama era of India, the Jewish era, etc."

He stood for the economic development of rural India and always gave vent to his feelings regarding various developmental schemes for the economically backward people living in a half-a-million villages. The provision of economic justice was his main programe. And this could be a achieved, he opined, if the colonial rule came to end. Indeed he got himself well-engaged in revolutionaries activities, but unluckily he died in 1939 before our country became free.

APPENDIX I

GENEOLOGICAL

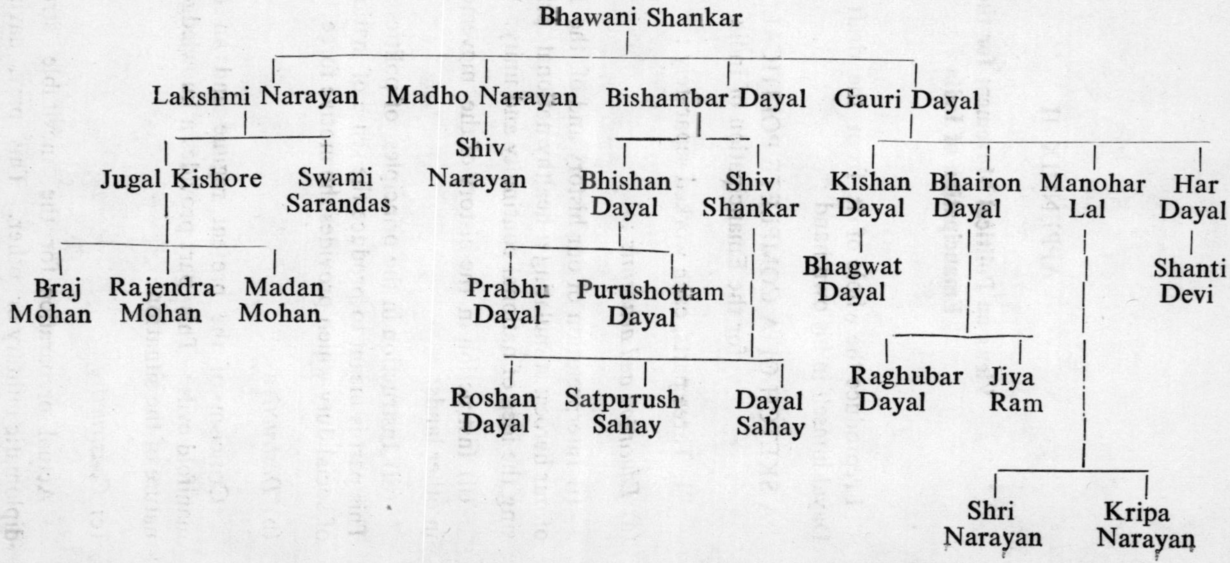

APPENDIX II

Views on Political Movement for the Emancipation of India

I reproduce the whole of it from the draft by Lala Har Dayal himself in his own hand :

"A SKETCH OF A COMPLETE POLITICAL MOVEMENT for the Emancipation of India

"I. Three parts, each worked separately :

(a) *Education and academic* :

(i) Interpretation of our history and of the lives and deeds of our heroes; stimulating a healthy national pride by impressing the idea of national continuity and unity.

(ii) Instruction in the history of the movements for liberty in other lands.

(iii) Instruction in the principles of politics and economics. This part is meant to produce the sense of national unity and of social duty which provides the motive force.

(b) *Destructive* :

Criticism of the present regime and an exposure of its manifold evils. This part provides a knowledge of the critical nature of the situation.

(c) *Constructive* :

Actual preparation for the inevitable struggle whether diplomatic military or other. This part, having formed the man, deals with measures.

"II. *Members* : Members are of 4 classes :

Desa-sarvasewaks (dedicators) :) Admitted to all the 3
Desa-sewaks (missionaries) :) parts at once.

Desa-sarvasawaks give up all wealth, and lead a life of celibacy and poverty.

Desa-sewaks give all their time and do not earn any money for themselves. They may or may not accept a small allowance from the Society and may contribute to the funds of the Society if they can.

Desa-premiks—enthusiastic members.

Desa-hitaishis—ordinary members.

The two latter classes may be admitted to either of the parts (a) and (b) or to both, but not to part (c).

Ladies can be admitted to all classes except that of married Dase-sewaks.

"III. Organisation : For

(i) Desa-sarvasawaks) A council consisting of all. President
and Desa-sewaks.) is elected. President has supreme executive power under the rules.

Funds under their control :

1. Fund for their maintenance.
2. Fund for the publication of literature.
3. Fund for part (c).

For (ii) Desa-premiks and
Desa-hitaishis.

Each premik shall have a sahayak of the desa-sewak or sarva-sawak class to assist him in his work for the cause.

Each premik will be sahayak to one or more hitaishis for the same purpose.

Functions of a sahayak are : (i) To assists his mitras (friends) in their work for the movement.

(li) To communicate to them all information regarding the movement which is supplied to him by his sahayaks.

"IV. Method of Admission : A member should first make sure of the zeal and knowledge of the candidate he wishes to propose. Unless he has reason to believe that the gentleman will willingly join any part, he should not disclose the existence of the Society to him.

He should send his proposal to his sahayak, who will submit it to the Council of the whole Society, composed of all the desa-sewaks, desa-sarvasawaks, one elected desa-premik for every 10 premiks and one elected desa-premik for 25 hitaishis. The election shall take place in the Council, which may delegate its powers to a committee.

"V. All work shall be quiet, with the exception of an Annual Assembly protesting against the various temporary and permanent acts of injustice perpetrated by the Government.

It should be carefully noted that private conversation and personal influence are the chief means of spreading an idea.

No news regarding the movement shall go into the newspapers, except the proceedings of the Annual Assembly and such measures undertaken by the Society as do not appear political in their nature, but are really meant to subserve a political purpose."

The aim of this Society, the object of his affection, was as clear as day-light. Har Dayal put it succinctly: "Actual preparation for the inevitable struggle, whether diplomatic, military or other." The method was "complete self-dedication," as he himself put it in his letter of April 15, 1907.

Was it to be a secret society ? "The Method of Admission" lays down that "a member should first make sure of the zeal and knowledge of the candidate he wishes to propose. Unless he has reason to believe that the gentleman will willingly join any part, he should not disclose the existence of the Society to him." Again, there was this addition; "All work shall be quiet. . . . Private conversation and personal influence are the chief means of spreading an idea. No news regarding the movement shall go into the newspapers, except the proceedings of the Annual Assembly." Those who have no experience of an organisation of this nature will perhaps jump to the conclusion that it was a secret movement. I would like to say it was a quiet movement. If the proceedings of its Annual Assembly could go to the Press how could the movement or organisation be called secret ? Of course it was not to work in that manner for all time to come. Har Dayal himself in one of his letters (Oxford, July 8, 1907) remarked : "I believe we must work quietly till we are a strong and well-organised party which can withstand any amount of opposition."

It appears that there were to be two parts of the Desa-bhakta Samaj or the Society of Political Missionaries. The second was to be given the name of Desa-sewak Samiti or Missionaries' Executive Committee. The object before this could not be different from the one before the Society. Still it was made clear : "The Samiti will have for its object the establishment of Home Rule on Swaraj in India. "The management of the Desa-bhakta Samaj was to be in the hands of the Executive Committee.

The principle of dissociation was necessary for the members of this committee also. It is stated in the rules :

> "No member of the Society will accept any titles, pension, office of emolument or hononary dignity whatever from the British Government or any other non-Indian government outside India except with the consent and approval of the Samrakshaks (patrons) and Sewaks."

Again, this also was to work quietly :

> "It shall rest with the Sewaks and Samrakshaks to make public or to communicate to the Sahayaks as much of the work of the Society as they consider expedient."

Another thing worthy of note is that religion as such was not given any importance, so that any person of any denomination or religious sect could be its member. Similarly no distinction was made between the two sexes. "There shall be three classes of members (without any distinction of sex or religion)"—this line given in the very beginning is, therefore, very important.

I give below the whole thing as it was drawn up by Har Dayal himself.

"DESH-SEWAK SAMITI (Missionaries' Executive Council)

"(1) The Samiti will have for its object the establishment of Home Rule or Swaraj in India.

"(2) Membership : There shall be 3 classes of members (without distinction of sex or religion) :

(i) Samrakshaks (patrons).
(ii) Sewaks (missionaries).
(iii) Sahayaks (assistants).

A samrakshak will be elected by the sewaks.

A sewak will be elected by the sewaks with the approval of the samrakshaks.

A sahayak will be elected by a sewak and approved of by the other sewaks.

"(3) (i) A samrakshak will be elected by sewaks on account of his services to the cause and his position.

(ii) A sewak will satisfy the following conditions :

(i) He will have to follow an adequate course of political studies and to live with a sewak for some time.

(ii) He will have no personal property whatever.

(iii) He will receive bare maintenance for himself and family from the Society. The education of his children will be provided for by the Society.

(iv) He will carry out the policy of the Society in accordance with the directions of the Executive Council of the sewaks, so far as the latter do not conflict with his conscientious convictions.

(iii) A sahayak will promise to abide by the rules of the Society and to give it financial and other assistance.

"(4) ORGANISATION :

1. (a) Samrakshaks will elect a President or Secretary for calling meetings or transacting other business. The Secretary will also communicate with the Secretary of the Executive Council of the sewaks.

(b) He samrakshaks will guide the general policy of the Society and receive a general annual report of the work from the sewaks.

II. The sewaks will elect secretaries for different departments of work and also an Executive Council composed of these Secretaries and others. The Executive Council will be the means of communication between sewaks and samrakshaks.

III. Sahayaks : The sahayaks will form themselves into groups or mandalis, and each of which will have a sewak or a gentleman nominated by a sewak for its secretary. The secretary of each group will receive the financial and other contributions of the group to the Society and will help the sahayaks in their work on behalf of the cause.

"(5) Rules: (i) All property etc. of the Society will rest in the samrakshaks and sewaks who together will form the Antarang Sabha (Inner Committee).

(ii) No member of the Society will accept any title pension, office of emolument or honorary dignity whatever from the British

Government or any other non-Indian government outside India except with the consent and approval of the samrakshaks and sewaks.

(iii) The sahayaks will receive a General Annual Report of the work which has been approved by the sewaks and samrakshaks (or Antarang Sabha).

(iv) It shall rest with "the sewaks and samrakshaks" to make public or to communicate to the sahayaks as much of the work of the Society as they consider expedient.

"(6) No alteration in the Rules of the Society can take place without a 9/10ths majority in the Antarang Sabha".

The political Missionaries' Society was actually formed in 1907. Persons like Pandit Shyamaji Krishnavarma, Lala Har Dayal and Mr. Sardarsinghji Rewabhai Rana were associated with it. One of the meetings held in London on December 28, 1907 discussed certain important things concerning the Society. The agenda must have been pretty heavy that day as the minute written by Lala Har Dayal in his own hand shows it.

We have to bear in mind that the building of the India House in London was bought by Pandit Shyamaji Krishnavarma for more than a hundred thousand rupees. When the Desabhakta Samaj was founded he passed it on to the Samaj. Besides this he donated rupees ten thousand.

Now we read the "Minute" which is a very important document because it throws light on so many facets of the life of Har Dayal.

"DESHBHAKTA SAMAJ

"Minute on the India House.

"(i) The management should be in the hands of a Committee as arranged previously.

"(ii) I have to go now, as my wife's residence in this country involves an enormous waste of time and money on account of her being liable to hysteria and on account of my friend's non-fulfilment of his promise to aid.

"(iii) As regards my returning immediately (from India to England) to manage the House and complete my political education.

(a) Whether it is expedient. I have already expressed my opinion that the India House is an important institution. In India, I can work among students and enter on the "best" life earlier. But I must first finish my Text Book before beginning active propaganda and a stay in England furnishes the best opportunities for this work.

(b) Whether I am ready to return. I am. I should stay only 3 or 4 weeks in order to meet supporters of the cause and arrange for the distribution of literature in the future.

(c) *Expenses* : Mr. Rana says, he or other friends are ready to make everything easy. Besides, my expenses may come out of the management if there are five or six people. Now I think that.

(i) I should pay for my board along with the others. As any surplus that may accrue will go to Panditji (S. K.) and I also receive help from him, it's all the same. If I live at the expense of other boarders, my moral influence is weakened and any defects in the management may be ascribed to a desire on my part to get a margin for my maintenace. I wish to appear as an equal member of a mess, not as a manager of a boarding house. Thus it is proper that I should pay £ 1.1s. weekly into the accounts.

(ii) I do not wish to trouble Mr. Rana or other friends as their money can be used for better purposes and I do not wish to put anyone to extra expenditure on my account. It is always matter of great responsibility to put others, especially the party, to great expense.

(iii) If a plan can be devised by which I can live here for a year without putting any persons to extra expenditure, I can return about the middle of March.

My father-in-law pays my pasage money to India now and I can get a return ticket at a small additional cost. I shall not trouble the party for this at present.

52 weeks at a guinea a weak would cost £ 54.

The return passage at the end of a year would cost £ 14 (deck).

Part of the money will of course appear in the surplus, if any accrues.

If it is considered proper, Mr. Krishnavarma may offer me a Lectureship for which I may be considered a deserving candidate. The sum of £ 66 would be just sufficient. If I can obtain any money from any other quarter, I shall went less out of the Lectureship for my personal needs. I shall keep Mr. Krishnavarma informed of my expenses and receipts as I do not want anything beyond what is necessary.

Thus all extra expenditure will be avoided as the Lectureship has to be offered to somebody. As Mr. Krishnavarma had intended to give me Rs. 1,000 till July, of which I have already received about Rs. 275, there remains out of that sum about Rs. 725 (£ 48) which I shall not want, now that I return to India. This circumstance may be taken into consideration.

(iv) *Furniture* : At least six bedrooms should be furnished according to the standard indicated by Mr. Master. This is a sine qua non of reform, which sho uld be guaranteed if my return to England is to be fruitful. We want more carpets, easy chairs, towel stands, pictures, etc. An estimate of cost should be prepared.

December 23 (1907). Har Dayal."

Glossary

Ahimsa	peace
Aman	non-violence
Badshah	king
Bania	member of the business community
Bapu	father, name often given to Mahatma Gandhi
Bhang	an intoxicant
Bhangi	a seavenger
Bharat	India
Cnamar	a leather worker
Charkha	spinning wheel
Chapati	thin, flat, unleavened bread
Crore	unit of measurement which is equal to ten millions
Dal	association
Darshan	sight of a venerated person or deity
Desh	country
Dharma	religion
Dharna	a sit-down strike
Ghat	bank of a river
Goonda	hooligan
Goondaism	hooligonism
Guru	teacher
Hakumat	rule

Hartal	stoppage of work
Himsa	violence
Islam	Mohammedanism
Inquilab	revolution
Istri	a woman
Jai	victory
Jalsa	a public procession
Jamait	an association
Jatha	numerous persons
Karma	action
Karmayogi	practical worker
Khadi	hand-spun and hand-woven cloth
Khalifa	head of the Muslim community
Kisan	a peasant
Kist	an instalment
Lakh	1,00,000
Lathi	stick
Lota	utensil
Mahatma	a high-souled person
Mahila	a woman
Murdabad	down with
Nari	a woman
Purna	full
Raj	commonly used for British rule in India
Sabha	a meeting
Sainik	sepoy
Samaj	an association
Sarhad	frontier
Satya	truth
Satyagraha	non-violent resistance
Satyagrahi	one who practises satyagraha
Seva	service
Swaraj	self-government

Taluka	revenue division
Thana	police station
Vakil	a lawyer
Vidyapith	an institution of higher learning
Yuvak	young
Zalim	cruel
Zamindar	landlord
Zamindari	landlordism
Zindabad	victory

Index